SALES IS EASY IF YOU JUST KNOW HOW

A PRACTICAL GUIDE TO CREATING MORE SALES IN YOUR BUSINESS, DOING SALES THE RIGHT WAY.

CHARLIE DAY

authors
AND CO.

CONTENTS

ACKNOWLEDGEMENT

To everyone in The Entrepreneurs Growth Club who has supported me every step of the way; I wouldn't have written this book if it wasn't for each and every single one of you.

INTRODUCTION

SALES THE RIGHT WAY!

I have built four businesses from the ground up. I launched the first business when I was 21 and I learnt really early on that sales were going to be the thing that moved my business forward. The sales in my business were going to allow me to have more choices, and grow and scale my business to the next level. Sales are the most important thing in any business, because if you don't have any sales, you don't have any customers... and if you don't have any customers, you don't have a business at all. So, if you aren't already, you should focus on creating a sales strategy that works time and time again, that creates sales whilst you're sleeping, and that you can rely on. If you already have a sales strategy that works, fantastic, let's take it to the next level.

I feel sorry for sales though, it's got a bad reputation over the years, and when I stand up and announce myself as a sales expert, people wince, 'oh no! What's she going to make me do?' Sales has become icky and uncomfortable and something people actively avoid. People say they don't want to be too pushy, or desperate, or in your face. Unfortunately, I have seen people come into the online space and use scarcity marketing tactics, dodgy tactics, sleazy closes or pushy methods, and this is why sales has got the bad reputation that it has.

I am here to change this.

I don't think sales should be any of these things. It's about solving peoples problems, it's about listening more than talking, it's about asking questions, serving your customers and making sure they have a great experience with you from start to finish.

You know when you've been in a sales situation and you feel great about it afterwards, you're glad you made the purchase... that's how I want all of my customers to feel after buying from me, and by using my proven sales method, this is how your customers will feel after buying from you.

Let's work together to change the face of sales. Let's make it something people love, and something we are all proud to do.

When you have finished this book, I want to hear you shouting from the rooftops about your business and what you have for sale, I want you to be looking for opportunities everywhere and having the courage to ask for the sale, and creating raving fans who buy from you time and time again.

I hope by the end of this book, you will love sales as much as I do.

LET'S GO ON HOLIDAY TOGETHER

I have an analogy, that selling and travelling on an aeroplane are similar! Stick with me, I promise you'll love this! When we begin with our sales, we are scraping around for sales, trying to get attention on our product or service, and trying to get noticed! It's a bit like travelling in economy, there are lots of people around you, and you have to work hard if you want anything! But if you are invited into business class, there is a serious shift; people are coming to you and asking you what it is you have on offer, you can recline your seat a bit, and although it still might be uncomfortable at points, it feels a whole lot easier! Now take this one step further and we are in first class, fully reclined and with your eye mask on. People have to come to you, and at the right time, if they want to buy from you. You are in demand and everyone wants to buy what you have on offer! And before long, you're flying on a private jet, and people can only buy from you when you step out of the plane and announce that they can, and oh my gosh, are they ready to buy when you do that!

When I announced this analogy to my community, they were on board with it straight away (pardon the pun!). Although a lot of them commented that they felt like they weren't even on the plane yet, let alone in economy! So, I made a promise to them; if they came into my world, I would get them in first class or flying on the private jet before long. If they listened to me, took my advice on board, and were willing to take massive action, they would do it! And I have had the incredible privilege to watch members of my community go from passport control to flying on a private jet, and the best thing is, you can do the same!

You might think I've well and truly lost the plot, but here's the thing, people are often put off by a book about sales, thinking it'll be boring, and about numbers and processes and using a whole load of jargon they won't even be able to understand, but not me! I am going to break it down by talking about flying on planes and going on holiday. It's going to be fun, you're going to get it, you'll have breakthrough moments, and you'll realise, SELLING IS EASY!

My promise to you is that I will teach you how to create sales in business the right way, with integrity, with the customers' best interests at heart and so you can sleep at night. You won't find me talking about any scarcity marketing, sleazy sales closes, or dodgy tactics. You'll find me talking about serving your customers, solving problems, listening, and going above and beyond for your customers.

So, are you ready? Do you want to go on holiday, me and you? Do you fancy it? Well, maybe not, because we have only just met, but I promise by the end of this, you'll be ready for a holiday with me, and not only that but you'll be able to have as many holidays as you like, as sales will be flowing to you easily.

Imagine that. I do love a holiday, and a holiday where I got to chat business and sales with you would be my idea of heaven. Shall we do Australia? We could feed kangaroos, visit Bondi Beach and watch a show at the Royal Opera House, or perhaps you fancy the Maldives? Snorkelling in the crystal clear waters? Sipping cocktails on a sand dune and spotting dolphins in the distance? Who am I kidding? You've picked up this book, so you probably want to do Disneyland? Let's go and see Mickey Mouse and ride the teacups and eat a dole whip! You choose! I can't promise it's going to be a smooth ride but I can promise you that we will get there. By plane of course! So kick back and relax as the fasten seatbelt sign is about to be illuminated and I'm going to show you how you can grab yourself a first class ticket, or even better, we will fly there on a private jet!

You don't believe me, do you?

You were already a bit sceptical about this book - after all, can one book really teach you how to sell? Can this book actually transform the sales in your business? Is selling really easy?!

The answer to all these questions - yes!

It's as simple as that. Yes! If you read this book you will go away knowing that sales is easy and you'll be able to go on the holiday of your dreams due to the sales you will achieve.

And how do I know? Because I've been there. I have been the person who has struggled to make sales, I have been the person hustling every hour God sends and have people looking at me thinking what on Earth is she doing, she's barely making a profit, and I have been the person so determined to show people that I WILL make sales despite what they think. I've been there, I know how you feel, I know that you've thought about giving up, not knowing what is the best thing to do - quit your business and give up altogether, or plough on in the same way you have, not making a profit. I have felt like this - lonely, clueless, and lost. And that's why I am here, to take you under my wing and teach you that selling is easy if you just know how!

Well done for picking up this book. This is the first step, and I promise if you follow the steps in this book, you WILL transform the sales in your business, you will go away from this book confident about your plan for sales. Sales will come easily, you will be a magnet for sales. In fact, problems that you might have in the future is that you will be so busy with sales that you will need to grow and scale your business in order to fulfil the demand (but let's not worry about that just yet)! I'm also going to give you my golden nuggets throughout this book, and just so you don't miss them, I'm going to highlight them as **GOLDEN NUGGETS** along the way.

I have spent the last five years honing my sales skills, and I have created a formula for sales success that I am going to teach you in this book. Please, don't be put off by sales! I know that a lot of people hear sales and run a mile. They think of a classic car salesman, a pushy estate agent, or cheap sales tactics used by telesales marketeers. Actually, this is the exact OPPOSITE of what I think a good salesperson should be. Selling should be about listening more than talking, sales is about answering people's problems and helping them see the solutions. I am all about doing business the right way. So do not panic, you're not going to be taught any scarcity marketing, sleazy selling, or pushy closing. It's all about selling the right way.

There are several components to an excellent sales strategy. We are going to look at marketing, honing and defining your message, creating the perfect pitch, building and nurturing your audience, following up, closing them down, and continuing to sell to them! We want to create raving fans, who buy from us time and time again, who shout about us, and who, in doing so, help us to make more sales.

When I have taken you on this journey, you are going to feel free. You're going to open the door to a whole new world of opportunity. Sales will come to you easily, it won't feel like an uphill battle, or that you are flogging a dead horse. You will have so many sales coming to you, your inbox will be full of enquiries and you will get to decide who you work with. I know that you will feel like this, because that is exactly how I felt. I was stuck but once I figured out how to open the door, sales flooded to me. I became a magnet for sales, I was fully booked, and it felt amazing.

If you are reading this and thinking, well is this going to be suitable for products or services? Is this suitable for big businesses, small businesses or medium size businesses? It doesn't matter - selling a pair of earrings for £10 or an online business for thousands of pounds - the fundamentals of selling are the same. I have helped hundreds of businesses, from Sue, who prints words on spoons for £10 a pop, to Lauren, who has sold thousands and thousands of pounds worth of franchises. I have helped Liz scale her bakery and sell her cookies across the world, and Jenna scale her PR and Blogging agency. I have helped thousands of business owners create more sales in their business, and I can help you too.

But who am I to tell you all this? Well, I have always been a dreamer. I remember my thirteen year old self, staring out of the classroom window in secondary school, dreaming of escaping, leaving the sleepy village in the middle of the Peak District where I lived, and moving to London to live out my dream of becoming an actress. Yes, that was my dream when I was thirteen. Despite people telling me it was 'never going to happen,' just three years later I was on the fast train to London to go to drama school. I couldn't believe it, it was all I ever dreamed of. I spent the next five years in drama school and I loved it, it was perfect for me. When I was twenty-one, I left drama school and entered the world of performing arts, and five months in, I decided it was not the job for me! It wasn't the life that I wanted, in and out of auditions, not knowing where my next job was coming from. I loved performing, but this life was not for me!

Thankfully, I have the world's most supportive parents so when I dropped this bombshell on them, they were understanding, and asked me what I was going to do next? Well that was a good question, what was I going to do next?

I would open a theatre school, the summer holidays were fast approaching and I decided that I could launch a little summer school during the holidays. Children would come for a week and perform a show at the end. I don't know if it was my twenty-one-year-old arrogance or my innocence, but I just assumed I would open a business and people would come flocking. I very quickly realised that this was not the case. I had hired costumes for 30 children, I had hired a huge hall with a stage, and I managed to get seven children there! Yes, seven children! Seven! I was working at a loss, and I had worked so hard. I was gutted, I was embarrassed and more importantly, I was losing money.

The week went well and I threw myself all in. I just thought at the end of the week, I will brush it all under the carpet and pretend it never happened. But something magical happened at the end of the week, every single parent who came said they were interested in doing more classes with me. At that moment, I thought to myself, "it was so hard to get these seven customers here, I'm not going to let go of them now", so I made a promise to myself at that moment. That I was going to learn how to sell, and I was going to be fully booked and that's exactly what I did.

That theatre school still exists today and is fully booked, with over 300 customers taught on a weekly basis.

I have gone on to build three businesses from the ground up, two of my businesses are franchised and I have over 60 franchises internationally. I have sold all of these franchises, and also assisted my franchisees make sales so that they are also running thriving businesses. I sold 30 franchises before I was 30 years old and I was awarded Young Entrepreneur of The Year for this accolade. I have built three multi-six figure businesses and at the time of writing this book, I am 33 years old.

I'm not just passionate about making sales for my businesses, I have helped thousands of business owners make millions of pounds of sales in their businesses too. I was also the top affiliate for the number one online launch in 2021, where I bought in over £120,000 for somebody else's business. And - wait for it - I got my first experience flying on a private jet, for my sales accolade and being the top performing affiliate. How crazy is that?!

You see, I am passionate about sales. I live and breathe it! But I have never had any formal sales training, in fact, I've never even had a 'real' job. So, if I can do it, you can do it too! Honestly, selling is easy! Selling is easy if you just know how.

And I am here to show you how. So turn the page, and let the plane ride begin!

2

YOU'RE NOT READY FOR THIS HOLIDAY

LET'S GET YOUR MINDSET READY

'Whether you think you can, or you think you can't - you're right'

— HENRY FORD

Before you go on holiday you have to get ready, and this holiday is no different. You have to think about how you think and feel about sales, your attitude towards sales. Are you holding yourself back? Are you standing in your own way? Are you putting barriers up in your sales process?

This quote that I have started the chapter with is one of my favourites, 'If you think you can, or you think you can't - you're right.'

It is down to you how many sales you make in your business, so if your sales are going really well, you can give yourself a high five as it's all down to you, but equally, if your sales are going down hill, that is also down to you. We are going to look at all aspects of your sales strategy in this book and I want you to be really honest with yourself about how well they are working. I want you to be open to giving them a tweak and trying new things and stepping out of your comfort zone.

I want you to go away from reading this book having unleashed the inner salesperson inside of you. My hope is that you will shout about your business from the rooftops, you will unapologetically solve people's problems in your sales process, and sales will come easily and naturally to you.

What you need to do to unleash your inner sales woman:

SAY GOODBYE TO NEGATIVE BELIEFS.

We are what we tell ourselves we are. Are you telling yourself stories around how good you are at sales? We are a combination of the top five thoughts that we have. We need to tune into those thoughts, listen to them, and understand if they are holding us back. If, for example, you are telling yourself 'I'm no good at sales, nobody is ever going to buy from me, I hate selling' or something similar, this is going to have a huge impact on your sales process, so we need to break down those barriers.

The first step is having an awareness of these thoughts, so I want you to start recognising common thought patterns that you have, write them down. That is the first step to changing the thought pattern.

Would you speak to a child like that?

When we write down those thoughts that we are telling ourselves over and over again, it can be quite shocking...

- I'm not good enough
- Nobody will ever buy from me
- Who do I think I am?
- I am fat/ugly

These are just a few thoughts that come up on a regular basis when I do this exercise with clients. Imagine if a child spoke to you like this. Imagine a child, maybe your own child or one you're close to, said 'I'm not good enough, nobody likes me, I think I'm ugly' or any of those negative beliefs we are telling ourselves. Instinctively, we would counteract that and say "no you're not, you're brilliant, you are clever, you are beautiful." We would work hard to change their thoughts on this, and prove to them they're wrong.

We need to treat ourselves with the same respect. We need to convince ourselves that these stories are wrong, and it is time we rewrite them. We need to become our own biggest cheerleaders and we need to realise that we can do whatever we put our mind to.

CHANGING THE THOUGHT TO A POSITIVE

The first thing we need to do when we have these negative beliefs is to write them down, acknowledge them, and then read it out loud. When we verbalise these things, it makes them real, and by saying it out loud you'll realise just how harsh it is. Then flip it. Literally change the thought from negative to positive. One thought I used to have was 'I'm not a good enough mum.' I thought because I didn't bake, or have limitless art and craft ideas, or my bag didn't have organisers in it, that I wasn't a good enough mum. But I changed that narrative. I'm showing my little boy that women can work and be a mum. I'm showing him that you can create your own business, build something from scratch, and he was there, watching me do it. It might not be the normal credentials for a mum, but I was doing it in my own unique way, so I changed the narrative. I am a good mum, and my little boy will grow up to be hard working, independent, and courageous because I showed him how. What narrative are you telling yourself? And how is this holding you and your business back?

LOOKING AT WHO IS ON THIS JOURNEY WITH YOU

Surrounding yourself with people who light you up, cheer you on and push you forward is absolutely essential if you are going to grow as a sales person and a business owner. We all have that one person in our life who is a bit of a negative

Nelly, who always sees the bad in a situation, and is guaranteed to bring your mood down. I am not saying that you need to cut this person out of your life completely, but, we are a combination of the top five people we spend our time with, so choosing to spend time with the ones who are excited about your life, your business and what you are building, is a really good idea. Even better if you can get into circles where people are a couple of steps ahead of you. They will push you forward, and make you realise you can achieve even more. Don't put a ceiling on what you can achieve, keep pushing the boundaries of your upper limits, and surrounding yourself with other people who do exactly the same is a really good idea.

CELEBRATING YOUR SUCCESS EVERY STEP OF THE WAY

Every Friday, I look back at the week just gone and I celebrate one thing that went well. Sometimes there might be more than one thing, but I write down at least one thing that I am celebrating. When we celebrate, we reflect on how far we have come, we are grateful for this journey we are on and how hard we are working. We also attract what we focus on, so if you focus on your wins, you will get more of them. I am at the point now where I have mini celebrations on a daily basis.

Another thing you can do to focus on your success is build a 'Yes I Can' wall. It's a great way to develop that positive inner narrative. Every time you achieve something in your business, be it a new goal, some positive feedback, an award, a good piece of PR, etc., you write it down on a post it note and stick it to a wall in your office. This wall is going to be called the 'Yes I Can' wall, because every time something gets too hard, or you think that you can't do it, you're going to go to that wall and remind yourself of all the absolutely amazing things you've done in your business so far, and you're going to remind yourself that yes, you absolutely CAN do it!

And you really can do anything you set your mind to.

Back in 2019, I had a burning desire to learn how to run. I don't know where it came from, and I tried to shake it off but I couldn't. Towards the end of 2018, I had learnt all about goal setting and I was going to put it into action. On 1st January 2019, I set out on my running journey - just for context, at this point I didn't even own a pair of trainers. I have never been the sporty type, I was the girl who was never picked for the netball team, I was rubbish at it, and I hated it. So, I spent most of my teens forging my mum's signature on a sick note and signing myself out of P.E. But here I was, wanting to learn how to run. I set out on the first day and I came back two and a half minutes later, a hot, sweaty, out of breath mess. My husband (who is an ex professional ice-hockey player) couldn't believe the state of me. 'It's not worth it, Charlie. It's not even worth putting your trainers on for a two-minute run.' But I did. I continued with my two and a half minute runs all week, and when I had been doing this for seven days, I found that I could run for 5 minutes. I had doubled my time, in just a week! This was progress. If I continued, where would I be in a month's time? Six months' time? A year's time? So, I carried on, and after two months I could run 5k, and I did something so outside my comfort zone... I joined in with our local Park Run, and to my surprise, I loved it. I wanted more. I signed up for a 10k, and then a half marathon. I was pushing myself to new heights. Then in October 2021, I ran The London Marathon, and it really was one of my biggest achievements ever. I never in a million years thought I would be capable of running a marathon.

I learnt so much about business by learning to run. It got hard at times. I felt like giving up, and I had to remind myself to keep putting one foot in front of the other, don't worry about being able to complete 5k or 10k or whatever it was I was aiming for, just keep putting one foot in front of the other. Don't look at others and what they are doing around you, just focus on yourself and your own journey.

If I can go from being told I'm rubbish at sports and not being picked for the netball team to running a marathon, we can all do anything we set our minds to.

The last thing I think we need to embrace if we are going to unleash your inner salesperson: YOU WILL FAIL.

I am really sorry to be the one to break this to you but you will. I did when I was running. I had a 10k I had to finish walking, I had six weeks off due to an injury and I had two half marathons cancelled because of a global pandemic. And gosh, have I failed in business! I failed right at the beginning when I couldn't convince anyone to come to my theatre school, I've launched products that nobody bought, I have had launches that I barely made a penny in, I have had several legal cases that I have had to fight. But each time I have failed, I have got up that bit stronger and it's made me into the business owner that I am today. As long as we are always learning from everything we do, we will always be growing. So embrace it, you will fail along the way, but my gosh, will you fly as well.

Before we go any further though, let's start with the end in mind - do you have a vision of where you want your sales to be? Without a vision, how can we celebrate when we get there? So how many sales would you like to create? I usually work backwards from a financial goal and then work out how many sales that would be.

Write it down and put it somewhere you can see it every single day. I want to make five sales per day, or I want to make x amount per month. I guarantee, in a couple of months time you'll be upping it, as you'll already be achieving it.

Are you ready for me to show you how?

TAKEAWAYS

- Write down your negative thoughts and let's flip them into positives.
- Start creating your 'Yes I Can' wall.
- Create a vision for your sales

3

LET'S CALL A TAXI!

YOUR MESSAGING NEEDS TO BE ON POINT

When you think you know which direction you want to go in, start! Start before you're ready, start before you really know what you are doing, just start! People will talk about ideas, but the people who actually take steps in the right direction are the ones who will go far! People overthink things too much in business, and I have something to tell you, not everything you do will work out, not everything you do is going to be successful, you're going to fail at some things along the way, so let's dive in feet first and get on with it. Don't wait until it's perfect, because it won't ever be perfect, we've got so much to learn along the way.

Let's call a taxi to take us to the airport. This is the first step towards going on the holiday. Well, our first step in perfecting our sales strategy is getting the word out there, telling people what your business is all about, marketing, prospecting, advertising, call it what you will, but everyone and anyone needs to know about your business and what it is you have on offer.

Everyone from your mum to your neighbour, your 94-year-old auntie Ethel and your five-year-old niece. Everyone needs to know what you do!

Why? Well the more people who know about your amazing product or service and everything it has to offer, the more people who are going to buy from you! Simple as that. And if they are all shouting about you too, telling their friends, then they can help to spread the word, they can be like mini marketeers for you. We want to create raving fans who buy from us time and time again, but they don't only buy from us, they also shout about us too. If each of our customers brought in another customer, our business would grow and scale organically. How amazing would that be? That's what we are aiming for.

Here's a nugget:
Make sure you're nailing your messaging so it hits your ideal client.
We need to make it clear, concise, and compelling.
Why do people need to buy from you?
What results are they going to see?
How is it going to make them feel?
How will it improve their everyday life?

I want you to think about another business that does this really well, it can be a small business that is similar to you, or a much bigger business. When I show up at events where we all introduce ourselves, I always see who I think has the clearest message, and the way I measure this is by thinking of the business I would be most confident standing up and introducing myself - they are the person who has nailed their messaging.

And less is ALWAYS more in these scenarios. Don't go trying to use all these fancy pancy words - make it clear, direct, and to the point. In fact, you'll really know that you have nailed your messaging when you can tell someone exactly what you do in less than eight words.

I want you to think about some of the businesses you love and buy from. Look at their messaging. I bet you it's simple and straight to the point. Make sure that yours is too. We want to make it crystal clear what we are selling, so that the right people buy from us.

How are you going to make it crystal clear to your target audience that what you have to offer is going to be of interest to them? Keep it simple, keep it clear, keep it direct!

'I help business owners create more sales so they can grow and scale their business.'

As simple as that. If somebody stumbles across my messaging

and they are a business owner wanting to make more sales (and let's face it, what business owners aren't!) then that messaging is going to jump out at them, they are going to want to learn more. If they are employed, or a stay-at-home mum, that messaging isn't going to speak to them at all, and that's great because they're not my target audience, so they can keep scrolling.

An easy way to do this is by writing down what it is that you do, how you can help, and WHO you can help!

The WHO is really important. Who is your target audience? It's really easy to fall down the trap of, 'oh, I'll sell to anyone, man or woman, old or young, business owner or otherwise, I'm not fussy, I just want the sale!' **We need to go narrow to go deep**. We need to identify who exactly our audience is, so that we can use our time, our marketing budget, and our organic reach wisely to draw the right person into our sales funnel. When I am talking about the 'ideal client', they are exactly that - 'ideal'. We might find that some people come along who don't fall into this bandwidth or 'ideal' and that is absolutely fine, we will still sell to them (if we feel they're right!). Another way of thinking about your ideal client is, who would you pay to be in a room with? If I gave you £1000 to spend on marketing, who would you get in front of?

The brilliant thing about understanding who your ideal client is, once you've understood who they are, you also know who they aren't. We've all been in that situation when we are selling and we are trying to fit a square peg into a round hole - they aren't the right customer, they've caused us problems before they've even bought from us! They aren't the right customer for us, but we are desperate to make sales so we are trying to make them the right customer. Stop right there and walk away. These customers will bring you problems as they're not right for you. They'll be more hassle than they are worth, and your time is much better spent drawing in your ideal client who will love what you have to offer, who'll shout about it and bring more customers your way.

Which brings me nicely onto, where does your ideal client hang around? Where do they shop? What newspapers and magazines do they read? Do they have kids? Are they home-owners? Where do they live? What do they love? How much disposable income do they have? These are just some of the questions I ask, if you want to download my full ideal client checklist then you can do so at;

charliedaysales.com/downloadables

Once you know the answers to all of these things, you'll have a better idea of what you need to say or do to get in front of your ideal client. Do they prefer consuming short sharp videos or do they like reading blogs? Which social media platforms do they hang out on? What are their biggest problems?

If you can identify their biggest problems you are well on your way to selling to them.

What keeps them awake at night?

What problems can you solve for them?

Sales, in its simplest form, is your ideal client having a problem that your product or service can solve. You are going to act like Cupid and marry the two things together, making it a no-brainer to buy from you.

For example, I imagine you've picked up this book because you want to make more sales in your business. You might even love sales, but you want more sales in your business. Maybe you've honed your sales skills and you're fabulous at selling, but you would still like more. So you see my book and you decide to grab it - why not, it's not expensive. So, I have these pages to show you that 'Selling is easy if you just know how' and if you get to the end of this book and you've implemented what I have told you to, and you've seen results, then at the end of this book it's going to be a no-brainer for you to come and find out how you could work with me further and I could help accelerate the sales in your business.

And that's what you have to do for your customers! Give them a taste of how you are going to solve their problems. Bring them into your sales funnel by showing them what you have on offer, give them value, solve small problems for them, build their trust and you'll have them coming back for more!

If you can position your messaging so that it solves your ideal customers' biggest want/need, it will make it a no-brainer for them to buy from you. This is why your messaging is so important, and we need to make sure you have nailed your messaging before we even worry about your marketing.

Once we have nailed the messaging we can put into place a marketing plan to help you get those sales in. Once people know what it is you have on offer, who it is for, and how you'll solve their problems, they'll be begging you to buy it, and the sales are going to come flooding in.

I want you to think about what is working at the moment. What are you doing in order to get the messaging out there? Write that down. What is working?

And then, I want you to spend one minute brainstorming what other things you can do in order to get your message out there. Go right now. Set a timer, don't overthink it, just put them all down on paper.

If you need some help, you can download my 50 free marketing ideas. Just go to

https://charliedaysales.co.uk/downloads

When you have done that, I want you to think about something that would really work to get your message out there but is impossible - maybe it's an advert on the TV, a billboard, or a huge spend on social media ads, but right now, it seems impossible. Write it down.

And then write down something that you've tried because you thought it would be a great idea, but it didn't work. For example, we tried for 18 months to get into newspapers before we did, and once we did, it was like we had opened the floodgates. They all came in, local newspapers, national newspapers, radio stations, the lot! So, do revisit those things that you know should work, but they haven't worked yet!

And this is how you should build your marketing plan:

- What works, you want to keep doing this!
- Brainstorm new ideas - what can you do that people aren't doing? Keep innovating!
- Keep trying things - your marketing efforts won't necessarily work straight away!

As a general rule of thumb, I do one in every five posts as a sales post, the key is to make them not look like they are selling - you know that they are a sales post, but the reader doesn't. Think about how you can hook the reader in, make them think that you are talking directly to them. I have five hooks that I use when I get stuck writing good sales posts:

How will it improve their average day?
What results will they see?
What problem does it solve?
How will it elevate their stature?
How will it make them feel?

Use these to grab their attention and hook them in.

I've got a golden nugget for you, I'm not sure if you're going to like it, but it's a nugget none-the-less, so I need to share it. Once you have found something that works, you need to rinse and repeat it, rinse and repeat, rinse and repeat. If it ain't broke, don't fix it!

This is where I see people come unstuck, because it's boring! Doing the same thing over and over is boring! Yes, it might be boring, but you're going to see results. So, fall in love with the hustle, master the mundane. Other people will get bored along the way, but we know that we will see results. So, once we've figured it out, we are going to keep doing it, until it doesn't work anymore, and once we get to that place where it doesn't work anymore, we are going to figure something else out that does, and then rinse and repeat it all over again.

Because we are committed to making more sales!

TAKEAWAYS

- Nail your messaging
- Narrow down your ideal client
- Create a marketing plan for your business, starting with what is working already and then adding in new ideas.

4

WE'VE ARRIVED AT THE AIRPORT!
FINDING VICTORY BEING VISIBLE

My dad always said to me: 'you've got to bang your bin lid' and it's stayed with me from when I was seven and he first introduced it to me, to now when I am building my empire.

Even if you have nailed your messaging, know who your ideal client is and where they hang around, you're going to have to work relentlessly to get that message out there. You're going to have to keep telling people, over and over again! And when you think you've spoken about it so much that you're going to burst, someone will say to you 'I didn't know that you did that!' And you'll have to do it some more.

Another nugget for you: facts tell and stories sell, so you've got to get your story out there in a big way.

Your story will stay the same, you'll just tell it in different ways, because what resonates with one person won't be the same thing that resonates with another person. So the message stays the same, but the stories around the messaging will change.

For me, it's all about sales. I can help you create more sales in your business, doing things the right way, with integrity, and with your customers' best interests at heart, so if that's what you need help with, then hello, I'm here to help!

I tell so many stories around this, how I left home when I was 13 and never looked back as I had ambitions that I couldn't bottle up, and I had to chase my dreams. I tell people how I learnt to run and I was terrible but I ended up running the London Marathon. I tell people about when I was a going to America but I had forgotten to apply for a VISA, so I used my super powers to get one super fast. I tell stories of bad sales experiences, good sales experiences, people who've inspired me. I talk about my love of holidays, and Disney, and musical theatre. I tell people about the struggles I had when I had my little boy as I had no idea how running a business and having a baby could work together. I talk about my husband and how he is also in sales and we have conversations about sales targets and converting customers and all sorts of geeky stuff.

All of those stories come back to one key point! Selling is easy if you just know how. And I can show you how!

I don't know how I ended up as an entrepreneur, I really don't. I come from a normal family, my mum and dad, my brother, two sisters, and then me. Most of the females in my family, including my aunties, had become teachers. Both my dad and my brother were employed (I call this having a normal job), but there was something about me that was never going to be normal! And I mean that in the best way possible.

One question I get asked a lot is how come you ended up doing this, who inspired you? The truth is, I don't know. Growing up, I didn't know a single person who ran their own business. It was never on my agenda. But what my parents taught me was that you needed to work hard no matter what, and that you had to bang your own bin lid. Nobody was going to notice you if you were shy, if you didn't stand up for what you believed in and tried to fade into the background! I took this and ran with it. I was the main part in all my school shows. I had the opportunity to perform on stages as a child, and I loved it, it lit me up. Even now, as a business owner, I am not afraid of trying new things, doing things differently or standing out from the crowd. I think this saying has done me proud, and now I'm going to pass it on to you. Let's get you banging your bin lid.

What can you do that others aren't doing? If we do what they are doing, we will blend into the background, be another one of the same, but if we are to make a huge impact so that we can create the sales we want, we need to shake it up a bit, we need to stand out.

One of my favourite quotes ever is: 'If you always do what you've always done, you'll always get what you've always got.'

So what can you do that's different?

Let's think outside of the box.

We already established in the last chapter who we want to attract, where we will find them and what message we are going to use to attract them.

Now I want you to think about what makes you different.

People buy from people, so you need to identify why people will buy from you!

People buy from me because I break it down. I make it easy to follow and I let people know that anyone can do it. I have no sales qualifications, I am not some big wig who has trained in corporate, it's just me. I started my business at 21, with nothing, no experience, no leg up, no customers, nothing, and I've learnt everything I know along the way.

I remember in the early days, I would get up in the morning and my then boyfriend (now husband) would leave for work and I had to create things to do. I had no emails to get back to, nobody to call, nothing that needed to be done, so I used to get out of bed each morning and create traction, create things that would get my business out there in a big way.

When I set up Charlie Day Sales, I started thinking about what my customers really wanted, what would make them stop in their tracks and listen to me? I know! Everyone wants more eyes on their content, how can I do that? How can I get more traffic to my ideal customers' content? I sat with it for a few days, and then I had it - #workingmumwednesday was born. Every Wednesday I would shout about other small businesses and share the hashtag #workingmumwednesday. I turned it into a game to see how far I could get it across the internet. The first week, nine people joined in. I wanted to gamify it but I didn't want it to be subjective, so I decided to turn it into a massive game of BINGO; each person who joined in got a number and at the end of the day I would pull a ball out of my bingo machine and whoever's number it was, the winner and would get featured on my feed. It went down really well. People came back week after week, people told their business buddies about it and it grew, and within months I was reaching my capacity of 90 (there are only 90 balls in my bingo machine!).

The other beauty of it was I could reach out to people. I used to message people saying; 'Hi X I see you're a small business owner and I wanted to let you know about #working-mumwednesday. Each Wednesday I share any mums in business on my Instagram stories and shout about your business to help get more eyes on your page. I'd love for you to join in on Wednesday. Love Charlie.'

Now, just a word about cold messaging: I don't agree with cold messaging, I don't think you should do it, I don't think it gets you anywhere if you are selling. But if you are cold messaging people offering them something completely free of charge which does more for their business than it does for yours, then, and only then, will you see traction in reaching out to people who you haven't spoken to before.

Golden nugget: cold messaging is a waste of time. It's annoying and does more harm than it does good.

Instead, think about what you can do for them. What have you got that your ideal customer would love, and lead with that. What is in it for your customers?

That's what I did with #workingmumwednesday. I started with the customer first, but in time, I ended up with more eyes on my business as everyone loved it, everyone shouted about it, and we created an amazing community. So I got more visibility, which resulted in more sales.

Surprise your customers. Do things differently, be courageous and try new things.

My husband is the worst at keeping secrets, he couldn't surprise anyone if he tried. He would always let the cat out of the bag about presents he had bought me, and throwing surprise events is just off the cards for us as he can't keep a secret. One day in the summer of 2014, I was having afternoon tea with my sisters and my husband was in London. I was supposed to be meeting him later on that evening, but half way through the afternoon tea I got a call. He was outside the restaurant. I was so confused as to why he was here, I ran outside and he was as white as a sheet on the other side of the road. I crossed the road without looking. 'What's wrong?' I asked him, my mind racing around and thinking of the worst scenarios that would have caused him to turn up looking like this. He grabbed my arm and pulled me around the corner. I was standing in between two wheelie bins in a car park of a local solicitors which was empty because it was the weekend. And at that moment, he bent down on one knee and asked me to marry him! I burst out laughing, what an emotional rollercoaster! It had probably only been two minutes but it felt like half an hour. 'Did I surprise you?' he said. 'Well yes, yes you did.' I had always dreamed of him proposing to me in a hot air balloon, or on the Amalfi coast, not in a bin store in Chelmsford. But I was surprised and I will always remember it.

How can you surprise your audience? How can you do things differently? I mean, maybe not proposing to them in a bin store, but you get my sentiment.

Conversations = sales. So let's get chatting.

We live in a world where people need around 60 micro touch points before they buy. That's not saying you won't get the occasional bluebird who ends up on your website, clicks through and buys straight away. But more often than not, you'll have to build and nurture that relationship before they buy.

In all three of my businesses, I have always focused on being as visible as I can be, building an audience, getting them excited about what I have to offer, creating a community, and then making sales.

I have sold birthday parties, theatre workshops, preschool classes, franchises, courses, memberships, journals, books, t-shirts, water bottles. And no matter what I am selling, the same rules apply.

Are you being as visible as you possibly can be to your audience? It doesn't matter how big your audience is, what matters is that you are showing up consistently for them. People get all wound up in how many followers they have, but what I like to focus on is how many sales I have. If you have 100 followers and they're all buying from you, then it's better than having thousands of followers but no customers. Trust me, I've worked with business owners who have a huge following, but have no sales strategy in place and struggle to convert them.

So, let's focus on sales.

Do you know who your super customers are? They are like gold dust and you must hold onto them. They are the ones who buy from you all the time, the ones who recommend you to others, who shout about you. These customers will act as mini marketeers for you, and are worth their weight in gold, so nurture them, thank them, make them feel as special as they've made you feel.

Do you know who your warm leads are? I have a list of warm leads at all times. These are people who send me strong buying signals as they're active in my communities, ask questions, message me, chat to me. A while ago, I told my community, The Entrepreneurs Growth Club, about this warm leads list and it's become a bit of a running joke. People will say to me 'put me down on your warm leads list, Charlie', but knowing who is keen means that you can continue to nurture those relationships, help them, give them value and solve their problems so that you are the obvious choice to buy from.

TAKEAWAYS

- Brainstorm stories you can tell around your business
- Identify what makes you different from the rest
- Create a warm leads list

5

WE'RE READY TO BOARD OUR ECONOMY FLIGHT

YOU NEED THE PERFECT PITCH

My husband won a holiday because he had made lots of sales for the company he works for. He got to take us with him and we were excited! There was a combination of work stuff and free time, they'd put on events, dinners and even hired baby-sitters for the kids. On the first night, we went down for a drinks reception. It was the first time I had met any of his work colleagues, and they greeted me with the dreaded question, the question every small business owner avoids - open up ground and swallow me up. And on this particular occasion I wasn't expecting it at all, which made it even worse....

'So, what is it that you do, Charlie?'

'Erm, well.... Now that is a question, well I sort of, mostly I am looking after our little boy really, have my own business too, you know, a bit of this a bit of that.'

Just because you run your own business, don't apologise for it.

Shout it from the rooftops, loud and proud. I help business owners create more sales in their business.

There are not many things that leave me speechless, but this is something I have battled with.

Mums in the playground, old family friends, husband's work colleagues. The only people I used to feel really comfortable really shouting about it with was other business owners.

It might seem small, but actually, this moment is someone asking us to do our pitch, and any opportunity we get to deliver our pitch we should grab with two hands and make sure we absolutely nail it.

Your pitch should be clear and to the point - don't fluff it up. The best sales copy will be easy to digest and simple to understand. In fact, if you can say what you do in less than eight words you will know that your messaging is so clear! When I started as a sales expert, I would trawl the internet for people looking for sales advice. I knew I had so much to give, and I knew I had to find those people who wanted it, so I would search and search for people who were looking for it. When I found them, I would give them loads of value in the hope that they would follow me and ultimately work with me. Since doing this, I have continued to get my message out there, that selling is easy if you just know how, and I am here to show you how. And now, if people see people needing sales advice, looking for someone who needs help with sales, they'll mention me! I am the person who comes to mind for them, but that's only because I have repeated my message over and over again. You need to be your own biggest cheerleader, shouting about why people should buy from you. But we also want to create raving fans, who shout about us and spread the word for us. You shouting about your business is one thing, but another person shouting about it speaks volumes! And if you can create an audience who does this, they'll be like mini marketters for you. If each customer you have brings in another customer, your business will grow without you even needing to try, and, as we know that leads are hard to get in the top of our sales funnel, we are going to chase after these personal referrals, which are much easier to come by.

SO WHAT SHOULD YOU INCLUDE IN A PERFECT PITCH?

Lead with what is in it for your audience. So often, I see people start a pitch with their name, who they are, information about themselves. What the people are interested in is how this can impact them - what change will it help them to see? What problems does it solve? If you can lead with this, it's going to hook your audience in and they're going to be more convinced to stay engaged for the rest of your pitch.

Now, if you are doing a short pitch, you are going to want to dive into what transformation you can show them, what results they will see, or how they will feel after buying your product or service.

Then finish with who you are, business name and a reminder of what you do.

Here is mine for reference:

'Do you want to create more sales in your business? Do you want to feel more confident about the sales in your business? Do you want to grow and scale your business?

If so, I would love to get to know you and your business more as I believe that selling is easy if you just know how, and I am here to show you how. I want you to feel like sales come easily and naturally. I am all about doing business the right way, with ease, confidence and integrity. You won't see any sleazy sales tactics here!

At Charlie Day Sales, I transform your sales strategy so that you can get more customers.'

It's as simple as that, no fluff, nothing extra, clear and to the point.

This pitch is perfect for opportunities where you have a 20-second pitch, sometimes people call it an elevator pitch - that is the length of it, you could give your pitch in an elevator journey.

Notice that I start with a question, in fact, I start with three. Questions are a great way to hook your customers. I call this technique 'The Yes Method'. The idea behind it being that if we can get our customers to say yes, they are hooked and open to buying from you. By saying yes, they are getting excited and we are raising their emotions and giving them a strong physio-logical response. If we can get our potential customers to feel these positive emotions and hook them in, then they'll certainly be listening to our pitch.

If you have the opportunity to give a slightly longer pitch, let's say you need to give a 90-second pitch - which is great if you are on a stage, or at an event, where people often specify exactly how long your pitch can be - so for those 90-second pitches, you can add in a story.

As I mentioned in the previous chapter, 'Facts tell and stories sell'.

It is so true. I often see people trying to tell by just stating the facts, but actually, if we can draw our potential customers in with a story, if we can make our customers think, and feel, and show them that others have felt the same way, they will be more compelled to buy.

I tell stories all the time;

- How I went from not owning a pair of trainers and hating any type of fitness or sport, to running a marathon
- How I tried to get to America without a VISA and had to manifest one
- The story of me starting a business at 21 with no clue what I was doing
- My husband proposing to me in a bin store

- How one of my mastermindees went from earning
  £3k per month to 28K a month after working
  with me

Just to name a few! Most of the stories aren't related to sales at all, but they all draw the reader in and I actually link all of them back to sales. I have a list of the stories I can tell and if I am going to speak at an event, I will take one of these stories and add it in.

I want you to write a list of the stories that you can tell. Give yourself 10 minutes and brainstorm all of the moments in your life that you could tell as stories now.

When you're putting your story together, you need to think about the structure. All good stories have a beginning, a middle, and an end. Your story doesn't need to be long, mine differ depending on which one I am telling. Go into detail in one aspect of the story because we want to make our listeners really feel something, so draw upon the emotions you or the character in question felt. And if you can either teach them something or show them a transformation, you'll be on to an absolute winner.

THE YES METHOD

As mentioned above, I have a method that I like to call "The Yes Method", which works really well when incorporated into your pitch.

When I was in Los Angeles, I was chatting to a lady about this method and she told me a fantastic story about a tramp who was well known for earning lots of money from passers by. He would sit outside a pharmacy on the corner of a street, and to everyone who came by he said 'are you going into that pharmacy?' The idea being that if you can get a yes out of someone straight away, you've got an in for a conversation.

My Yes Method is similar! If you can ask three questions consecutively, that the answer is yes to, then you'll have hooked the potential client in. You'll see me doing this a lot, I love to lead with questions, and as a good salesperson, we should be asking questions all of the time.

So, for example, I often ask;

'Would you like to make more sales in your business? Do you want to grow and scale your business? Do you want to feel great about the sales in your business?' If the answer is "yes", then you are in the right place, because I can show you how.

My ideal clients are small business owners. Most small business owners want to create more sales in their business, and grow their business, but they want to sell the right way, without being sleazy or icky. So these three questions work really well to hook my ideal client in.

Think about your ideal customer and what three questions you could ask them, which the answer would be yes to, which would make buying for you a no-brainer.

THE IMPORTANCE OF A PITCH

When you are pitching, you are showcasing you and your business, illustrating who you are and your credibility. If we are going to buy from you, you need to be confident, sure of what you are offering, and trustworthy. You need to get that over in your pitch. I mention this now because I have heard people include in their pitch:

'This is really cringey'

'I hate doing this'

'I am really nervous'

It is fine to have all of these feelings, but you absolutely cannot include them as part of your pitch, as it's not going to instil confidence in you and your brand. Take a deep breath, and go in confidently and courageously.

FEEL THE FEAR AND DO IT ANYWAY

Too scared to pitch? Ask yourself, what is the worst that could happen? Go there, imagine that the worst thing does happen... is it that bad?

Each time we put our pitch out there, we get better at it, we see what works, what lands well. Remember, practice makes perfect so the more you do it, the better you'll get.

Make sure you get your energy in the right place because you don't want to be delivering a lacklustre pitch. One trick that I do is do ten claps and then do my pitch, this gets your energy up. This is much easier on a Zoom call, if you are in a live networking event, you might want to take yourself off to the toilet to do your ten claps.

Don't be afraid to be you. Show up as your true self, be unapologetically you. If people don't like you, then they're not the right people for you. If you are always showing up as your true self then you'll attract the right people, so just be you.

THE MORE YOU SHOW UP, THE MORE YOU'LL BE SEEN

Set yourself a challenge, I am going to give my pitch at least twice a day, at least ten times a week. Get yourself out there, in front of new audiences, switch things up, experiment, and get yourself heard.

I love nothing more than listening to people pitch their businesses - as you've probably realised already, chatting to small business owners is my favourite thing, so, if you're feeling nervous about your pitch and you want to practise, feel free to follow me on social media and send it over.

TAKEAWAYS

- Write a 20-second pitch
- Write a 90-second pitch
- And practice, practice, practice

6

STEPPING ONTO THE RUNWAY

BUILDING AND NURTURING YOUR AUDIENCE!

We have made so much progress; the foundations of your sales process are well underway and we can really move to the next stage. Let's step out onto the runway and head onto the plane. I think we are ready.

But before we go any further, we need to make sure that our audience that we are growing, know, like and trust us! Why should they buy from us? Why are you the obvious choice? And why should they buy your product or service and not your competitors?

Set yourself apart from the crowd. Why should people buy from you? What makes you different? Let's start there. Write a list of things that make you different, things that make you stand out from the crowd. Why do people love buying from you? Why do people buy from you time and time again? What do people say about you?

Nobody is you and that is what will make your business different.

If you're racking your brain thinking, what DOES make me different? Know that people will buy from you because of YOU! Nobody else is you, so they could be offering the exact same thing as you are, but they would still be different as they are not you. In this world we live in, where we are building a business and a reputation online, the more you can let that shine through, the better. The more you can show **you** and how passionate you are about your business, the better.

People in the online world often talk about showing up as your 'authentic self' and it really winds me up - what does that even mean? How can I show up as my 'authentic self'? So, I thought I would outline some ideas:

- Go live: show people behind the scenes, a day in the life of, get yourself in front of the the camera and show them who you are
- Share with them what you love: your family, your hobbies, what you love outside of business (Only ever share as much as you're comfortable with)
- Talk from the heart: don't be afraid to stand up for what you believe in and share thoughts and opinions.

- Tell stories: people love to see the emotions you felt in certain situations and understand what you have been through, to get to where you are today.
- Have fun! : Fun reels, silly stories, interact with your customers and potential customers... just have fun with it.

Remember, not everyone is the right customer for you, and that is fine. Understand when someone isn't the right customer for you, and walk away from them, or even better send them to someone else who is perfect for what they are looking for. It is an excellent skill and one that you need to be a top salesperson.

When I first started in business, I didn't do this and it was a huge mistake. It actually does more damage than good. I used to try and fit a square peg in a round hole, and those customers who aren't a good fit are usually the ones who cause more problems down the line, so walk away and move on, you won't regret it.

When we are building up the trust of your audience there are a few things that we need to think about, and it doesn't matter if you are selling online or offline, the same rules apply. However, I do think every business should be building an online presence regardless of if they are only operating online or running an offline business. We live in a world where people average out at 60 micro touch points before they purchase, so we have got to get our message out there and let people know what we are all about before they will buy from us.

WHO IS YOUR AUDIENCE?

This is your ideal client. We have recognised that they are the people that want and need the product or service that you are selling. We have created messaging that is going to stand out and speak to them. We recognise exactly who they are and what they need.

WHERE ARE YOU BUILDING YOUR AUDIENCE?

Whether it is online or offline, you need to know exactly where you are building your audience. There are so many options: on social media, on an email list, in a group. It's great that there are so many options, but don't be too overwhelmed by that. I recommend that you focus on one main platform or group to grow your audience. For me, it was my group The Entrepreneurs Growth Club, which became a hub for small business owners to share business ideas and problems, and to support each other and cheer each other on. Even now, I link everyone back to there. It's such a great community and I am always giving hints and tips on how to create more sales in your business. This a place where people can get to know me, understand the way I work and see if they like it.

Think about where you can build your audience.

HOW DO YOU WANT YOUR AUDIENCE TO FEEL?

This is one of the most important things, but it's often overlooked. How do you want your audience to feel? If you start building an audience just to make money, just to make sales, that will shine through and people will be able to see that. You need to think much bigger than that. How do you want to make people feel? What change do you want to see for them?

For me, I want people to go away from working with me feeling more confident about the sales in their business, feeling empowered. I want to impact millions. I want you to read this book and go away feeling more confident and motivated to move the sales in your business forward.

CONSISTENCY IS THE KEY

You've got to be consistent, getting your message out there consistently, and sharing five main themes of your business. Don't change those themes too much as you want to be known for one thing, so as soon as you come to mind, so does your message. Or, even better, as soon as someone is looking for the thing your business is all about, your name comes to mind. For me, if anyone is looking for help with sales, I want to be the person who comes to mind. What is that for you? And how can you choose five themes that help get that message across? My five themes are: sales, marketing, growing and scaling a business, being a woman in business, goals.

Be consistent. How often can you show up for your audience, on a daily basis? How often are you providing them with content, with videos, with lives, with interactive content? Don't let them forget about you, get their eyes on your content.

When I started my theatre school and later on, when I ran Phonics with Robot Reg, we used to offer free trials - you could come along for a class to see if you liked it before committing to a full term. This model really worked for us, until it didn't anymore. Before long, everyone was offering free trials, so much so, that you could go to a different class every week for free and fill up your whole year with trials, so we changed to paid trials and they worked better. We grew a business on this model.

We want to try before we buy, whether that's trying a new chocolate bar that they hand out in the middle of the train station, a new preschool class, or an online business, we want to get a flavour for what it is we are buying. Social media has given us such a great platform to do this, especially service-based businesses - use it wisely. Give people value, give them a taster, lure them in with your expertise, your passion, your energy. You can show them what it is you have on offer and leave them wanting to buy from you.

Ask them what they want and deliver on that. People love to be listened to, to be understood, so ask your audience - what do they want to see more of? What do they love? What makes them happy? How can you help them?

Build a community. People love being a part of something, and if you can make people feel as though they're a part of your business, they will love it. They will feel so invested in it that they will stick around.

As a family, we go to Disney a lot, and my husband found this a little strange when he first came into the family - if you weren't brought up going to Disney, it's a lot to get your head around. But Disney gets it so right. They make you feel part of it, which is why you have people of all ages, demographics, and backgrounds, dressing head to toe in Disney, queueing for hours to see Mickey Mouse, and coming back time and time again for more.

How can you do it in your business? If you are in my community, The Entrepreneurs Growth Club, you'll know you can catch me every Sunday at 8pm going live. You know I will comment on your post if you use #theentrepreneursgrowthclub, and you will be a part of my business and the decisions I make. You're a part of my communitty. I have been stopped by members of The Entrepreneurs Growth in the middle of London, in my hometown, and even when I was in the middle of the sea on The Disney Cruise. I love it! I want to meet as many members of The Entrepreneurs Growth Club as I can. I wouldn't be where I am today without them, I am where I am because of them and we are all on this journey together. I celebrate with them each week:

I celebrated when I was in the top 10 podcasts, I celebrated with them when I was named top affiliate in the biggest launch in the UK, and I celebrate their successes on a daily basis too.

Running a business is about more than the money and the freedom; it's about the difference you can make in the world, and the change you could see. People think because I am always talking about sales that I am driven by money, but I am not. I want to change the face of sales for female entrepreneurs. I want female entrepreneurs to sell with courage and confidence and do it unapologetically. When I talk to more female business owners who love it, and want to shout about what it is that they do from the rooftops, than I do those who hate sales and find it icky and uncomfortable, I will know my work here is done.

What is that for you? What is the change you want to see? Tell your audience, share it with them, and let them be a part of the journey.

Look after your audience and they will serve you, they will be good to you, and they will help you to create even more sales. Do not underestimate the power of your audience. Often I hear people saying 'if I just had more leads I would make more sales,' 'if there were more people in my audience I would make more sales.' Don't focus on what you haven't got. Yes, it is always important to be growing your audience and getting more leads into your sales funnel, but you do already have an audience, so look after them, serve them, and they will become raving fans, who not only buy from you time and time again, but also shout about you.

TAKEAWAYS

- What makes you different?
- What value can you offer? Make a list of all the different things you could share with your audience.

7

WE ARE STEPPING ONTO THE PLANE!

CREATING REAL RELATIONSHIPS

Now is your big moment. You've made it this far, you're ready to step onto the plane.

I have learnt in building all of my businesses that community is everything. Walt Disney once said; 'People spend money when and where they feel good.' We want people to feel a certain way when they buy from us, we want them to know that we will go the extra mile for them, and we want them to feel great in doing so. If we get this right we will create raving fans who buy from us time and time again, and that is what we are aiming for. If each customer that came into our business loved it so much that they spread the word to family and friends, they would bring in more customers. And if each customer bought in another customer for us, our business would grow and scale without us having to do anything. And that is why we have to create real relationships with our customers.

What can you do for me?

As customers, we are single-minded. We only care about one thing, and that is ourselves. We go into transactions thinking, what can they do for me? And the better businesses are at fulfilling that need, the easier it will be to get us to buy. Selling, in its simplest form, is a person having a problem, want, or need, and a business having a product or service that solves that problem or feeds into that want and need. We have to use our messaging and positioning to marry these two things together and hey presto! We have ourselves a sale. But how are you going to do that? How are you going to use your messaging and positioning to make it a no-brainer to buy from you? That is the question.

First of all, ask questions. The more we can understand their wants and needs, the more likely they are to buy, so ask questions, ask lots of questions. It doesn't matter if you are talking to them on the phone, face to face, email, or Messenger, start asking questions from the first enquiry. When we start asking questions, often the replies can be surface level, so I then go on to ask further questions, uncovering their bigger problems. I think of the customer like an onion, we need to peel back all the different layers to really get to the centre of the problem.

For example:

'Hello, I would love to enquire about your sales course. I am absolutely terrible at selling, and could really do with some help.'

Answer 1:

'Thank you very much for getting in touch, my sales course starts on June 18th and costs £9999. During the course, we will look at every single element of the sales process from marketing all the way to closing the deal and upselling further products or services. I would absolutely love to have you on the course'

The result to answer 1 is that they either buy or they don't buy. You could also try and follow up with them a couple of times afterwards to try and push them over the edge.

Answer 2:

'Thank you so much for your enquiry for my sales course, I would absolutely love to know a little bit more about you and your business, and what difficulties you are having at the moment with your sales process, and hopefully I can help you decide if this course is right for you or not?'

Response:

'Thank you so much for getting back to me, to be honest I am terrible at it all'

'Sometimes when we are in our business and feeling overwhelmed by all of the different aspects

it can be difficult to see where it is that we're going wrong. Tell me about a recent transaction that didn't quite go the way you wanted it to?

'Well someone was enquiring with me last week and then suddenly they just went quiet on me and never got back to me again or bought from me, I was really frustrated as I spent loads of time chatting with them just for them not to buy!'

'Oh gosh, that's so frustrating when that happens. I am sure that there are some tweaks that we could make in your sales process to encourage people to get back to you. Did you follow up with this potential customer?'

'Oh no, I wouldn't have known what to say!'

'I think my sales course will really help you. I think that we could definitely look at all aspects of your sales process and why people might be falling off that customer journey. We could also look at your follow up and what to say to potential customers if they do go cold on you, and also teach you exactly how to follow up. I know that these two things alone would have a serious impact on the sales in your business.'

You can see the difference between these two conversations, asking questions gives you so much more leverage to sell to them.

Leading with open questions is a great idea too because it gets the customer talking.

The more we can get them talking, the better as we can really start to uncover their problems and learn more about them as a buyer. Ideally, in the first half of your conversation with your potential buyer you should be listening 80% of the time.

If you are going to be an excellent sales person you will need to be able to listen actively. Your customer really wants to be heard.

Active listening is a skill, and it might take you time to master this skill, but I want you to start today. Active listeners avoid any sort of judgement, so you need to go into all customer conversations with an open mind. If you can, write down key words that the potential customer says to you, then repeat them back so they feel really heard. At the end of them speaking you can reaffirm what they have said, making them feel heard again. Not only will it make them feel heard, but it will also engage your brain so you are actually listening to what they are saying, and your brain will start to look for ways to solve their problems.

Active listeners also show empathy and aim to really understand how the other person is feeling, and put themselves into their shoes.

When we are asking questions and listening to our potential customers, it means that we are in a position to give them a personal experience. There is no cookie cutter approach, no copying and pasting answers or details, it's about having a new conversation with each potential customer, about feeding into their wants and needs and giving them a personal experience and really showing that you care.

Go above and beyond. This is what I always strive to do. I don't want to be doing what Sandra down the road does, I want to do what Sandra down the road DOESN" T do, as I know that's going to help me stand out from the crowd. Do things differently and go the extra mile and people will remember you for all the right reasons.

Where are your favourite places to shop? To eat out? To go on holiday? To spend your money? Where do you not mind spending money because it's worth it? For me, it would be Disney, John Lewis, my nail bar. They all go above and beyond and strive for excellence, and that is why I love them. I try to be the same for my customers, I want to be nothing short of excellent.

Know what makes you different, that is what will be your selling point, and you need to lean into that. You need to make sure it shines through on social media, in all your literature, and across your website. Be unapologetic about why your business is absolutely awesome and why people should be buying from you. These are your strengths. Equally, it is important to know what our weaknesses are, as these are the areas we need to improve, or outsource if we can.

'Those who ask will certainly receive.'

I recently went into my local nail bar. I have been going to this particular nail bar for ages. As previously mentioned, I absolutely LOVE this nail bar, it's got such a lovely vibe, there's positive quotes on all the walls, which is an instant tick for me, they give you a neck rest, and you can even get a glass of wine there. What's not to love? As I said, I have been going there for a while, the workers know me, everyone is lovely and friendly, and it's just all in all a good experience. Last time I went, as I was going to leave one of the ladies sheepishly came up to me and asked, 'I wondered if you could possibly leave us a Google review?' Now I had raved about this place to the workers and told them how much I loved it, so I said; 'of course I will' and they were really appreciative. They don't have a clue that I run my own business and I know the importance of a Google review, so I went home and immediately wrote it. It got me thinking though. Previously, had they just hoped that I might write a Google review and then when I didn't, ask me to? Maybe it was a meeting that morning where they were reminded to ask for reviews? Maying I am over-thinking it and the lady just saw her opportunity. Either way, if you don't ask you don't get. I know how important reviews and testimonials are, and still I wouldn't give one unless I was asked. We have to condition our customers to do exactly what we want them to. They're not mind readers, and even if, like me, they know the importance of reviews and testimonials, it still won't be at the top of their list to do one for you. Think how you can add it into what you already do. It could be asking people to give you a shout out on social media, asking for reviews, or asking to refer friends and family. It's not going to magically happen, we have to condition our audience to do this for us. If we are going above and beyond for them, they will go above and beyond for us.

If we can have every single customer shouting about us and what it is we do, and acting like mini marketeers for our business, it's going to help our growth and our sales.

Give yourself permission to be you, be unapologetically you. Your customers and everyone who does business with you will love it for you. The more you do this, the more you will find customers who are like you and are attracted to you. This will help you to create real relationships with your audience because they will see things in you that remind them of them-selves, or that they love, or that they resonate with, so commit to being one hundred per cent yourself.

TAKEAWAYS

- Brainstorm why your business is different from someone in the same industry/a competitor.
- How can you get your customers shouting about you and your business?

8

IT'S TIME FOR THE UPGRADE

CREATING YOUR OWN OPPORTUNITY

Ask and you shall receive!

I met my now husband in a nightclub in Clapham. I was recently single and I went with a small group of girlfriends who all dispersed as soon as we got there, to find the man of their dreams. As though that was going to happen at a nightclub in Clapham! I did a lap of the place, and to be perfectly honest, I wanted to go home. I wasn't in the right frame of mind to be at a nightclub, essentially by myself. At that moment, a guy came up and asked me if I could lend him one pound so that his friend could put his coat in the cloakroom. He seemed cocky and sure of himself, and I was very confused why he would be asking on behalf of his friend, was it a chat up line? I only had a five pound note, but I had nothing else to do and nobody else to talk to, so I said I would queue up with him and give him the pound. So I did. We realised we were both from the north - I grew up near

Sheffield and he was from Hull - and he seemed friendly enough. When we got to the front of the queue he said; 'I would offer to buy you a drink, but we probably won't see each other again now.' And him and his friend were off, and I was left on my own again.

I saw him at the end of the night. He was slightly more drunk, but he shouted 'Charlie, I owe you a drink!' Damn right you do. And so he bought me one and we chatted. And then when we left the nightclub he asked 'Can I kiss you?'

I have learnt a lot from my husband, but one thing I have always admired about him is his ability to ask questions. He asks questions all the time... which lead to opportunities.

If you don't ask, you don't get.

So, let's start asking for exactly what we want.

It's weird because even now, looking back at this story I think, what were the chances of meeting my soulmate on that evening in Clapham? If Lewis had never asked for a pound, I never would have met him. If his friend had just decided to hold onto his jacket for the night, we never would have. And if I hadn't said yes to giving him the pound, we would never have ended up being married. We create our own opportunities all of the time, and this is definitely true in sales; we are constantly creating our own opportunities.

Just so you know, the guy who owned the jacket was a witness at our wedding. I never did get that pound back though!

BE OPEN-MINDED

We need to go into our sales process open-minded. We don't want to judge ourselves or our customers before we have already started the transaction. An example of judging ourselves is telling ourselves we aren't good enough at sales, or this person is never going to buy from us, or that they're not going to pay that money for it etc... and an example of us judging the customer is this isn't going to be right for them, they'll want something different, or they'll never buy from me. Both of these things are going to impact the sale. You want to go into any sales calls or messages with an open mind. Be curious. Find out what they need and what their problems are and then decide how you are going to sell to them. You should go into every sales call with the knowledge that you can serve each customer or potential customer, that you have everything you need and that it will go well.

SAY YES! OR HELL YEAH!

If you go back to the story of me meeting my husband, if I hadn't been open and said yes, then I never would have married him! By saying yes, we open ourselves up to new and exciting opportunities. Now, as you scale as a business owner, you might not be able to say yes to everything - there just aren't enough hours in the day. But if there is something that excites you, something that feels like it's a good opportunity, even if it's scary, say yes.

BE PREPARED TO FAIL

What's the worst that could happen? Be prepared to fail. Every single successful business owner I know has failed somewhere along the way, and if you know one who says that they haven't, they're probably lying. Failing is all part of learning and growing, and if we are open to failing, it doesn't feel so hard when we do. Next time you are scared, ask yourself 'what is the worst thing that could happen?' It usually isn't that bad.

GO FOR THE NO'S

When I first started in business, all my selling took place on the phone. I grew to love selling on the phone, and even now, I find it much easier to sell on the phone than via Messenger/email. In the beginning however, I hated it. Absolutely hated it. So, I used to play a little game with myself. Each morning, I would set myself a challenge to go for 10 no's. I was cold calling schools and nurseries, and I would give them my pitch and if they said no, I would mark it off on my chart, and as soon as I had 10 no's I could mark it off on my chart. What happened along the way of me getting lots of no's is that ultimately, I would get some yeses, but this mindset shift is the reason I fell in love with selling on the phone.

STEP OUTSIDE YOUR COMFORT ZONE

Comfort is the casualty of growth, and I want you to be so committed to growth that you are fearless. If we want to be in the top 2% of salespeople, we are going to have to have the courage to step into unlimited sales success, and that's not going to happen in your comfort zone. Every day, just push yourself slightly outside of your comfort zone. Some days, you might just have your little toe out and on other days, your full body will be out. Slowly, over time, what you are comfortable with will be more and more, until you find it almost impossible to step outside of your comfort zone.

FLEX THE MUSCLE OF IMPOSSIBILITY

At the end of 2018, I found personal development, and it was love at first sight. It really unlocked something inside of me. I couldn't devour enough personal development books and podcasts. I attended seminars, training, and business conferences. Then on 1st January 2019, I set some goals. As I mentioned previously, the first goal I achieved was learning how to run. When I set out on my running journey, I didn't even own trainers, and the thought of being able to run seemed impossible at the beginning, but two years after my running journey started was when I really decided to flex the muscle of impossibility. A good friend of mine was diagnosed with breast cancer. She was just 32 and had three young children. The news hit me, I couldn't stop thinking about it, and as I sat in my office, I started to think about what I could do to support her. Nothing seemed enough. And then I decided I would run a marathon. The very thought scared the life out of me, but I knew it was nothing compared to what she was going through.

Training for a marathon is one of the hardest things I've ever done. It is long, it is boring, and it is monotonous. You get to the point where you just don't want to run anymore, but you have to, you have to get back out and running, you cover some serious ground during marathon training and it's hard. I just kept focusing on putting one foot in front of the other. Just putting one foot in front of the other is easy, there's nothing hard about that, so that's what I focused on.

When the race day came, I figured it would be easy. The crowds were huge and the energy was electric, only one problem - I had never run a marathon before. Even in training, I didn't get to the point where I actually ran a marathon, so I had no proof I could actually do it.

I remember at mile 22, I was so close to the end, my family were there and I stopped and leaned on the railings separating me from my family. 'There're only four miles to go,' they told me. Four miles seemed impossible. I felt like I couldn't do it, but I knew I had to do it. Towards the end, I actually got quite angry at people cheering me on shouting 'not far to go now.' To be honest, two hundred metres seemed far at this point, it was honestly the hardest thing I've ever done.

Reflecting back on my experience of running a marathon, I realise that I learnt so much. I flexed the muscle of impossibility. I honestly believed that running a marathon was impossible for someone like me.

Throughout this process, I didn't just learn about me and my capabilities, I also learnt so much about business. Here were my learnings:

- Putting one foot in front of the other will move you forward. Even if, at times, the steps forward are so tiny, you are still moving in the right direction.
- You will always feel like giving up, but you must never give up.
- People might be cheering you on, but you need to believe that you can do it.
- When it gets hard, put more energy in.

The biggest thing I learnt is that anything is possible if you put your mind to it.

What is that for you? What would you love to achieve? What have you always dreamed that you could do? The only thing that is stopping you, is, well you. Go out there, make a plan and achieve that goal, because I can guarantee, once you've achieved that thing that seems impossible, you'll realise that in fact, anything is possible.

To give another example of me flexing the muscle of impossibility, during the pandemic when we were all restricted on leaving our houses, I set myself a challenge to learn how to juggle. It felt impossible. I am so uncoordinated. I stood there on day one with just one ball passing it from hand to hand. Then, when I had got that, introduced ball two, and then three and four. It was a slow process, at times I felt like I was going backwards, but I persisted, and now, I can juggle. I flexed the muscle of impossibility.

SEEK AND YOU SHALL FIND

There is opportunity everywhere, it is up to you to go out and find it.

This year, I went to a two-day mindset immersion and I absolutely loved it. If you've got this far into my book, you'll probably realise that I am not 'woo' at all, and everything I talk about around sales is based on strategy and processes. However, one thing that really interested me that came up on this mindset retreat was this idea that the universe is here to guide you. I left the two days and found myself saying out loud, 'ok universe, if you are really here to guide me, show me a sign'. I was literally leaving the event to get my taxi home and just before I got in my taxi, I noticed a group of about five white feathers. Was that the sign? I pushed it to the back of my mind and climbed into the taxi. When I was back home later on I went for a walk, I said out loud, 'If a feather is a sign from the universe then show me another one' I immediately noticed another white feather. Was this manifestation or just coincidence? I kept noticing white feather after white feather, everywhere. I eventually had the courage to tell my husband what had happened, (I knew he'd think I'd lost the plot.) I told him the full story, and he was laughing, but as he laughed, guess what floated down from nowhere? A white feather! Even he thought it was a bit weird. Feathers have followed me everywhere since. I went to France and saw feathers, I went on a cruise ship and saw a white feather in the middle of the sea, I was inside a theatre and down floated a feather.

If you are reading this and think it's a whole load of rubbish, I get it. But I think we've got two options: either we trust in the process and think the universe is looking after us, or, we realise that if we look for something hard enough, we will find it, whether that's opportunity, sales, or white feathers. Seek and you shall find. Believe that it is out there for you, and it will show itself to you.

TAKEAWAYS

- Focus on what you want most: write it down, visualise it, believe it is going to happen.
- Set yourself a challenge to flex the muscle of impossibility. What can you learn to do that seems impossible?

9

TAKING YOUR SEAT IN BUSINESS CLASS

LET'S CLOSE DOWN THE SALE!

Why should people buy from you? And why should they buy from you now?

You are responsible for making it compelling for people to buy from you. Make it a no-brainer, make them so desperate for your product or service that they are waiting for the link to buy, going out of their way to purchase, or looking out for when it goes on sale.

It starts with you. You need a plan, without one your sales will be impacted.

As always, I recommend starting with the end in mind - when are you launching? When does this go on sale? When can people buy from you? And what is going to create urgency for them to buy? Perhaps you are going to add value, perhaps there are only so many spaces, it's a limited edition, the first people to buy will get something extra... You want to warm people up and get them ready, get them excited, waiting for you to release, so that when you do, they buy it because you've created that urgency. When you do this, it will be much easier to sell, so it's important to start thinking about the sale weeks before it actually happens, and plan for how you are going to release it, when you are going to release it, how you will create that urgency and how you are going to close them down.

I want to mention at this point, that when I talk about closing down, it needs to be coming from a good place, it needs to be true, and it needs to be done in the right way. It's more about being honest with your customers when we say, 'I've only got x amount of space', or, 'I am only taking bookings until this date'. Remember, everything should be done the right way, and with the customers' best interests at heart.

Closing is a key part of the sales process, but what I am really passionate about is that close being real and true, and a time bound compelling reason for them to buy your product or service right now. For example, I don't believe in saying you only have five spaces left and then when those five have sold then magically another fifteen spaces come available, or you're giving away something extra for the first five but it then suddenly extends beyond that. We want people to have trust in us and our brand, and the way we are going to do this is by doing things with integrity and selling the right way.

Examples of closes:

When I ran a party agency, we used to use dates as a closing tactic. We knew which dates were popular ahead of time, and we could only do so many parties per date, so that worked as a great close.

When I ran my theatre school and pre-school classes, we would use numbers as a close - 'we only have x number of spaces left'.

For my online business, I only open the doors at certain times of the year, and there are bonuses for buying early. If you miss when the doors are open, you have to wait. This works as the perfect close.

For subscription boxes, I would have a cut off date each month to work as the close.

For product-based launches, I would add extras in when launching new products for the first so many bought.

Whatever it is that you are selling, it is always worth thinking - why should they buy from me and why should they buy from me now?

BUILDING TRUST IN YOUR BRAND

Think about your favourite brands to buy from. Why do you love buying from them? One of the reasons will be because you trust them, you know what you're going to get, they're reliable, they are consistent, and therefore, they have your trust.

When you have that trust, people will buy from you time and time again. They will know that whatever you are going to come out with next is going to be good, and they will get to a point where they want to buy from you regardless of what you are bringing out.

But if you lose their trust, the opposite is true. People won't want to buy from you and it will be difficult to regain that trust and get them to buy from you again.

So, think about your consistency, your reliability, and your honesty when it comes to this part of your sales process.

I DON'T LIKE DISCOUNTS

People often use discounts as a close, and I'm going to be honest, I don't like discounts. We all believe that our product or service is worth having, we are all doing everything to make buying from us an amazing experience. So why would we discount it? I think discounts are given to things that people don't want any more, things that are out of season, out of fashion or nearly reaching their sell by date. That is certainly not how I want anything I am selling to be seen. So instead of discounting it, I think about what value I can add. I stand in the knowledge that what I offer is absolutely amazing, and if people don't buy it, they really will be missing out.

ASK QUESTIONS TO QUALIFY AND USE THE INFORMATION TO CLOSE

If you can make your closes personal, you really will be on to a winner. What I mean by this is, rather than just saying we only have five spaces left for that, instead, really understand the reason that people wanted to buy it in the first place. Why have they contacted you now? What made them get in touch with you? Why now?

My first ever business coach specialised in sales. He might have had something to do with why I love sales so much now. I met him at a business showcase, and I was so intrigued by everything he was teaching, I enquired how I could work with him. He asked me to set up a call with him and he would discuss everything on the call. So, the following day, I had a call with him. He told me a little bit about his mastermind, and I said I was really interested in joining (at this point I didn't even know the price). He asked me 'Why do you want a business mentor? Why me? And why now?' I spent the next 15 minutes explaining why I needed his services and why I needed them now. Then he told me the price! It was way more than I thought it would be but I was already in. At the time, I thought I was lucky that I found him when I did. But in reality, he sold it to me, and he sold it to me really well.

The more you know about why your customer wants to buy from you, and why they want to buy from you now, the easier it is to sell to them.

Also, I know phone calls are sort of old fashioned these days, but selling on the phone is so much easier as you can get people talking, and really start to uncover their desires. You have to work much harder to achieve this over direct Messenger, so if I can get them on a call, I always will. I also keep asking questions in emails and direct messages too. The more you know, the easier it is to close.

Opening sales calls with questions is such a great way to start understanding exactly what the customer wants. I open all of my sales calls with questions, it gets them talking and you can very quickly get to the good stuff - why they want to work with you, why they got in touch in the first place, and why they want to do so now. Write yourself a script for sales calls and put in as many questions as you can. You should only be talking to ask questions, and then to close them down. People generally love talking about themselves, so don't waste any time, get them talking.

You've got two ears and one mouth, use them in proportion. Listening is a key element to sales, you have got to be a good listener in order to create more sales, and so often I see sales people talk themselves out of a sale. A few years ago, me and my husband wanted to book a holiday to Florida to go to Disney. We knew exactly what we wanted, but I convinced my husband to book it with the new travel agent that had opened up near where we live. It was really swanky, the sort of place where you could get a latte whilst booking your holiday, there was even a kids area to keep them entertained whilst you book.

I went in and the lady asked me 'where do you want to go on holiday?'

'Disneyworld in Florida.'

Her face instantly lit up, 'we went there last year and had an amazing time, you don't want to stay there too long though, I would break it up and have a break in the middle. We went to a really nice hotel about an hour away for a few days in the middle for a beach break.' She pulled the hotel up on her computer and I interrupted her, "we were actually thinking of staying at a Disney hotel.'

'Oh, you don't want to do that, they're really overpriced for what they are. Why not stay in a villa?'

And so, the conversation went on. I sipped my latte, made my excuses, and left. We went in there to book our holiday, but her poor sales skills meant we didn't. I am sure the holiday she was trying to sell us was absolutely lovely, but it wasn't what we wanted. We knew exactly what we wanted, and had she asked questions and listened to the responses, she would have understood that. She should have found out our budget, what we were looking for, if we were going for anything special, and created a holiday especially for us.

As I have already mentioned, we are in sales transactions most days, so open your eyes and your ears to who closes you down well, and who doesn't even bother. When you can close someone without them realising, it feels great for both sides.

BE PREPARED TO DO THE STUFF THAT OTHERS DON'T TO GET THE RESULTS THAT THEY WON'T

We are really getting into the details of your sales process here, but if you put in this level of thought and detail into your close, it's going to separate you apart from the rest; it's going to put you in the top 2% of sales people in your industry and you will rise above your competitors.

We aren't just thinking about how to close the customer down for us to get the sale, but also because we want the customer to feel great about the purchase. You know those scenarios when you buy something and it just feels great! That's what we want for our customers, and if we line it up so we have qualified that they are the right person to buy from us, we have the right product or service for them, and now is the right time for them to buy, they are going to feel great about buying from us.

With this comes saying goodbye to the wrong customers. Don't try and fit a square peg in a round hole, if they're not right, they're not right, move on and find the next lead. Or, if now isn't the right time, give them some space and they'll come back to you. They might say they're thinking of buying in six months or a year's time. Great, put a note in your diary and reach out to them then. Great sales people wave goodbye to the wrong customers.

'THANK YOU' GOES FAR

It seems obvious to me, but since I can probably count on one hand the amount of business owners who thank me for my custom, I thought I would include this here. If someone buys from you, thank them, if they recommend you, thank them, if they shout about you, thank them. Remember, if we can get other people talking about you and acting like mini marketeers for you, you will make more sales. So throw thank yous around like confetti. Make people feel special and valued.

Here's a nugget for you: Remember that going above and beyond and doing things that other people aren't prepared to do is what got you your seat in business class. You don't want to lose it now.

TAKEAWAYS

- What close will work best for each thing that you are selling?
- Remember to ask questions to qualify your leads so you can close them easier.

10

SAFETY BRIEFING - FOLLOW UP!

If you only take one thing away from this book, let it be this - follow up! It's the most important part of the sales process. We could all do more follow up. And the more follow up you do, the more sales you will make. It really is as simple as that!

This should come with a warning, that's how important follow up is, so read carefully.

Here's a nugget for you: YOU CAN CREATE MORE SALES TODAY JUST BY FOLLOWING UP!

You should follow up with absolutely every single enquiry that comes into your business. If you don't, you will be leaving money on the table.

I follow up with everyone, current customers, past customers, potential customers, collaboration opportunities, follow up with a thank you for buying, thank you for recommending me, thank you for the testimonial.

I can count on one hand the number of small business owners that follow up consistently. People tell me that they don't want to come across as pushy, or too much, but whenever anyone follows up with me, I think it's kind. They've had the thought about me, they want to let me know what they've got on offer, they've sent me a personalised message, I don't ever see that as pushy.

If you are the type who thinks it may feel pushy to you, then I want you to think of it as part of your sales process, and just give it a go for 30 days. You'll see the results.

I actually think following up with everyone is key. If you go out for a drink with a friend, follow up and say what a lovely time you had, if you receive a gift, follow up with a thank you, and if you do business with someone, always, no matter what, follow up with them, and those people will come back for more.

I don't have time - this is the number one objection that I meet with when I ask people why they don't follow up. You must make time. You must make time because this is where you will make more sales, and therefore, following up is vital. Make time for it, factor it in, it is a non-negotiable.

SO, WHO DO I FOLLOW UP WITH?

Anyone and everyone.

You should definitely follow up with people who enquire about your products or services. Each month, I go back and I look at these people and follow up with them, even if they enquired a while ago. We still know that they are warm leads who are interested in what you have to offer.

Follow up with people who recommended you.

Follow up with old customers.

Follow up with current customers.

Follow up with people who are in your group.

Follow up with followers.

Follow up with people who are joining in with your challenges.

Follow up with people who email you.

Follow up with collaborations.

Follow up with press opportunities.

Make following up part of your daily routine!

I have a spreadsheet so I can keep track of my follow up, and I follow up immediately with someone after a sales call, and then after 24 hours, and a further 24 hours.

HOW TO FOLLOW UP?

Keep it simple and straight to the point. If I'm offering something new, I think of all the people who might be interested and tell them about it. I ask direct questions and keep it short and sweet.

'Hi Alex, I don't know if you've seen but I am doing a sales challenge next week, I'd love for you to get involved. Here is the link. Charlie x'

'Hi Alex, have you seen my new mastermind? It's specifically for people who want to make huge leaps forward in their business next year and I know you have huge plans for next year. Here are all the details, I'd love to jump on a call with you and discuss this further, Charlie.'

'Hi Alex, I know you were really interested in joining The Entrepreneurs Sales Lounge. We have an amazing training coming up on How to Create Extraordinary Success. Are you still interested in joining? Charlie'

WHEN TO FOLLOW UP?

When people get in touch with you, they are interested in your product and service at that very moment, and whilst we might not be on hand to answer their enquiry right away, we want to get in touch ASAP. Equally, if somebody has gone away to have a think about it, go back and follow up the next day. A day older is a day colder, the longer you give them to think about it, the colder they're going to get. You want to be having these follow up conversations on a daily basis.

I keep following up with people. We know that they're a warm lead, we know they're interested in what you have to offer, so keep following up, until you feel like you can't follow up anymore....

Follow up quickly and strike whilst the iron is hot to try and get that sale in.

THE BREAK UP MESSAGE

My process is to follow up three times, and if they all get ignored, I move onto the break up message. I really try to get people into the yes pile or the no pile, I don't want people sitting in the maybe pile for too long. Of course, we must give them the time and space to think about if they want to buy or not, but once we have given them the space, it is your job to follow up with them.

'Hi Alex, I've messaged you a few times now about joining

The Entrepreneurs Sales Lounge, I haven't heard from you so I'm guessing you are no longer interested? Charlie'

Have a list of warm leads, an ongoing list of people you can follow up with.

Feel the fear and do it anyway. What is the worst that can happen? Somebody might message you and tell you that they're not interested. That's great, at least you know, and you can move onto the next lead.

'I don't want to seem too pushy.'

'I'm worried they'll say no.'

'I don't want people to dislike me.'

Think about how you feel when someone follows up with you? We don't immediately hate someone for following up with us, often I am grateful as I might well have forgotten all about them. Remember, that customer is top of your list, but you are not necessarily top of their list, so keep following up. As long as it is coming from a good place, you genuinely think this would be great for this particular customer, it will be received gratefully.

Make this part of your routine. I sit down every Sunday evening and look who I can follow up with. I spend an hour following up with different people and different opportunities, then every morning I look at who I can follow up with. It is that important to me and my sales process that I do it every single day.

We all live busy lives, we have so much going on. I know that I often enquire about things that I am interested in and then forget about them. I move onto the next thing and forget about whatever I was buying, and then I see an email later, 'you abandoned your cart' 'you didn't check out on Amazon'. Oh, yes! I wanted to buy that thing. If we can automate some of the follow up in our business, even better! When someone follows me, or joins The Entrepreneurs Growth Club, I follow up with a message to try and find out more about their business. If someone downloads something, they'll get an email follow up. I have a chatbot that also helps me with follow up, but sometimes the follow up needs to be personal, and this cannot be automated, so I do recommend doing a combination of both.

Personal outreach goes hand in hand with follow up for me. Who can you reach out to who you know is interested in buying? Perhaps they've bought before, perhaps they've enquired, you know they're watching. Send them a personalised message and tell them what you have got on offer that they might be interested in.

Even if they don't buy, they'll remember you, you'll stick in their mind, and they may well come and buy from you in the future.

It isn't just potential buyers who we should follow up with. We should follow up with current customers, past customers, people in our community, people who want to collaborate...

follow up with opportunity, follow up with everyone. Yes, I know I am repeating myself but it really is important.

I want you to take a moment to think about your favourite small business owner, someone you buy from, you think they're doing a great job, and you love supporting them. Imagine that they send you a message right now telling you about a new product or service they had coming up and because you have been such a support to them, they wanted you to be one of the first people to find out about it. How would you feel? You'd probably want to know more. It's a business that you know and have used before, you might be quite excited as to what it is, because you've loved everything else that they've bought out. But also, you might feel touched that they have thought about you, and gone out of their way to get in touch with you and tell you about it. I don't think at any point you'd feel like they were being pushy, and even if you weren't interested, you would probably send them a kind note back just explaining why it wasn't for you. This is what we want to create when we follow up.

I was once sitting next to this fabulous lady at a business event I went to. She was an intuitive guidance coach and I had never met anybody who did anything like this before so I was intrigued. I was asking her all sorts of questions about what she did and how she did it. In the end, she said to me 'you should come to our two-day retreat that we are holding.' She told me about it and I said it sounded really interesting and asked her to send me the details. If I'm honest, at that moment

I didn't really think anything more of it. But then she followed up with me and when I looked at the details, it was only half an hour away from my house, and I could make the dates. What were the chances of that? I looked with even more interest at all the details, and I thought it was meant to be, so I booked on. Would I, without her following up? Absolutely not.

If, after reading this chapter, you are still nervous about following up, then go for the no's. Set yourself a challenge every single day to get 10 no's. Go and follow up with everyone and you can't stop until you get 10 no's. What will happen along the way is that you will get some yeses. You'll make sales along the way, but this mindset shift will mean that you are going for the no's, so it won't feel like a knock if you get any. Remember, following up is just a part of your sales process, it's not personal. If it's not the right time for a customer to buy, that is fine, it's nothing against you. Or if they are the wrong customer, or they need something else, it's not personal, move onto the next sale. Of course, if you are coming upon the same stumbling block over and over again, it might be worth looking into, but you also need to be aware that not every person will say yes, and that is fine. I bet you'll be amazed at the number of people who do want to buy from you when you start taking your follow up seriously.

Do not underestimate the power of following up.

TAKEAWAYS

- Make a plan for the follow up in your business
- Look at what follow up you can automate in your business.

11

WE'VE ARRIVED AT OUR DESTINATION

SO WHAT IS NEXT? ADDING AN UPSELL

You've done it. You've created a sales strategy that works. People are buying from you, and what is even better than that is they love it, they're raving about it, they want to buy more. It is our job as business owners to keep our ear to the ground and listen to what they want next, they've loved the first thing you offered them, what else do they want? And how can you feed into that?

This is why creating real relationships is key. We want to have that relationship where we ask our customers what they want to see next, what they would find useful? You need to be one step ahead of your customers and give them exactly what they need next.

Don't let it get to the point where they are moving onto the next thing before you've even recognised they need it and you could offer it.

SO WHAT DO YOU NEED TO DO TO CREATE AN UPSELL?

Well, first of all, the initial thing that you are selling to them has to be absolutely excellent and leave them wanting more. They need to feel great about what they have received from you and wondering what they can buy next.

We need to follow up with our customers about the upsell as soon as they come to the end and are ready to buy the next thing. Follow up with them and tell them what you have on offer, make it really clear and super easy to buy.

Or, if it's appropriate, you can even add an upsell when they're buying from you, like McDonalds' asking 'do you want to make that a meal', or Costa asking 'Do you want to make that the Columbian blend?' They're upselling to you. Can you do that to your customers?

Could your upsell solve a problem? How much do we love it when Amazon suggests things that you might like to buy based on other things that you've bought? How can you do that for your customers?

HOW TO UPSELL?

Understand what success is for your customer and help them reach it! The more you know about what your customers want, the easier it is to create that and then sell it to them.

If you are providing them with real service they will look to you for other things, so be laser focused on making sure that your customer has an amazing experience the first time that they buy from you.

Use social proof. If you have already built an audience that knows, likes and trusts you, bringing out other products will be easy to sell because the trust is already there. Not only will those people buy from you, but you'll also be able to use social proof to get others to buy from you too.

WHAT IS IN IT FOR THE CUSTOMER?

We live in a fast-paced world where people demand excellence. We have to keep up with the latest trends, what people want and need, and we have to put our customers' needs first. Before I put any offer out there, I always think 'what is in it for the customer?' Our customers are the reason we have a successful business, without customers we would have no business at all, so we owe it to them to put them at the heart of our business.

Think about how you want your customers to feel after they've bought from you, when they've finished working with you. I want my customers to feel amazing. I want them to feel as though I have empowered them to create more sales in their business. I want them to feel motivated and unstoppable, but I also want them to think it is easy and convenient. I start with that, and reverse engineer it. What would I need to do, what would I need to offer, how would I need to treat them, in order for them to feel like this at the end of working with me?

Some of the best companies that I use on a daily basis - Facebook, Deliveroo, Uber, Amazon - have put in so much thought about the customer and what they want and need, for convenience, ease, and efficiency. Again, as customers, we want things yesterday, and the leading companies recognise this and give us what we demand.

BECOMING CHOPPED LETTUCE

I always use chopped lettuce as the perfect example that there is always an audience that wants what you have on offer. Do you buy chopped lettuce? Or do you buy a whole lettuce? Chopped lettuce usually divides people, after all, lettuce is one of the easiest things to chop, and the mark up for pre chopped lettuce is 50% more than the whole lettuce, so why is it in demand? People like ease, they are health conscious and want to create a salad easily. There are some people out there who wouldn't dream of buying chopped lettuce; it's more expensive, it doesn't last as long, it doesn't taste as good, and it's bad for the environment. But there are always people who will buy chopped lettuce, and there will always be people who won't.

Two things to take away from my chopped lettuce analogy:

- People will always buy what you have on offer, but it is only right for a certain customer, and that is fine.
- People want ease and convenience. Are you offering that? Do you have a chopped lettuce product?

Whilst on the topic of chopped lettuce, it's worth mentioning pricing, as this is something that often comes up in the sales process. But as you can see by my chopped lettuce analogy, the price does not come into it at all when buying chopped lettuce. The people who buy it can afford it. If you are going to price yourself at the top end of the market, there will always be people who want to buy from you, but similarly, some people don't want to. It's all about recognising who is your ideal client and who isn't. After all, not everyone buys chopped lettuce.

CONTINUING THE RELATIONSHIP AND GETTING REFERRALS

When people have bought from you, it is essential that you keep that relationship going, because not only do you not know when they are going to buy from you again, but you also don't know when your name, or your niche is going to come up in conversation and you want to make sure that your name is on the tip of the tongue. We send birthday cards, emails, and personalised messages to keep those relationships going, even after they've been a customer with us. I also continue to follow up with past clients too for the same reason. Check in with people and keep those conversations going.

CONDITIONING OUR AUDIENCE TO SHOUT ABOUT US

People will not shout about you automatically. It is up to us to condition our audience to shout about us, to share, to comment, to like, to spread the word. I used to do this every day, sending personal messages to anyone who shared me, or tagged me, or just generally put in a good word for me, and before long, they did it without me having to try. But don't assume people are going to do it, and don't look at other people who are getting tons of shares and shout outs and think that they're lucky! They will have put in the ground work and got their audience to this point, and the great thing is, you can too.

If you want a testimonial - ask

If you want a referral - ask

If you want a shout out - ask

TRUST AND CONSISTENCY

I have already asked you to think about companies that you love to buy from. I can guess you love to buy from them because you trust them. On the other hand, I bet there are some companies out there that you won't buy from, because you don't trust them. Trust is everything. If we can build up that trust then people will buy from us in the future much easier. However, if we lose that trust... well, let's not even talk about that!

I recently stayed at a Hilton Hotel in New York. It's a chain of hotels I trust, but when I got to this particular hotel, it was grim to say the least - dirty and basic. And yet, it was one of the most expensive Hilton hotels I've ever stayed at. When I told them, they were unapologetic and said it was one of the most popular Hiltons as it's just off Time Square. I happen to know that Hilton Hotels are a franchise, and as an ex-franchisor, this is one of the problems many franchisors come up against - they haven't got that consistency across the brand and this is one of the reasons people might lose trust. Other franchised companies, let's take McDonalds for instance, you trust that when you walk in. It doesn't matter if you are in London or Bradford, Paris or Berlin, if you order a Big Mac, you'll get the exact same thing no matter where you are in the world.

Think about your business, is there consistency across the brand? And do you build trust in the customers because of this consistency?

TAKEAWAYS

- What is your upsell?
- Make sure it is clear and easy to buy.

12

LIFE ON A PRIVATE JET

MAKING SALES TIME AND TIME AGAIN

I have had the opportunity to fly on a private jet twice! I know, right, that's mad! From reading this book, you'll have realised I'm just a normal person. I've never had a real job and I've got no fancy qualifications. But what I have committed to is my sales strategy. I recognised early on that having a killer sales strategy would be what moved my business forward, and it has, in all of my businesses. Having a killer sales strategy has meant I have moved forward much faster than my competitors, who did not focus on that. I know that you will do the same. You've got to the final chapter of this book, so well done, congratulations. Now all you have to do is implement, take massive action, and never give up. The reason I had the opportunity to fly on a private jet twice, in case you were wondering, was also down to sales. I partnered with a fellow business owner, to create sales for her and her business. When I first partnered with her, there were incentives for the top sales people. I didn't take them in, I was just focussed on my proven sales strategy that works time and time again. I was completely shocked when I was top of the leaderboard and her number one salesperson, but even more shocked when she told me I would be flying on a private jet with her and a few others to enjoy a lunch in Barcelona. I couldn't believe it. I have been comparing making sales and flying for years, and I always dreamed what it would be like to go on a private jet, and here I was, going on a private jet because I had made sales. What a coincidence! Or was it?

Selling is energy, and we have to protect our energy with everything. The energy we put out into the world is what we get back. So, maybe I was putting out some private jet energy when it came to my sales strategy.

IT'S ALL ABOUT YOUR ENERGY

If sales is energy, you need to think about your energy and make sure it's in a good place to ensure it is working as part of your sales system. Learn about your energy and what you can do to get your energy in a good place before selling. For example, if you stand up on a sales call, your energy will be in a different place. I always put on some music and dance before I do a sales presentation or masterclass. Getting up each morning and proclaiming 'sales come easily' and 'I am a magnet for sales' gets my energy in the right place for the day ahead. Having an excellent morning routine and going to the gym, and looking after myself also gets my energy in the right place to make more sales. If you're sluggish, not feeling good and have low energy, it will affect your sales.

When you have just made a sale, your energy is in a good place too. You want to make another sale, and you should go out there and get another one in the bag with that energy. However, when you get on that downward spiral, you're not making any sales, your energy is in a bad place, you start to doubt yourself and your product or service. When you are there, it is difficult to pull yourself up and get into that upward spiral of making sales all the time. So we have to protect our energy and make sure it's in the right place for creating an abundance of sales.

TAKING MASSIVE ACTION

So, there you have it, my seven steps to sales success:

- Marketing and messaging
- Building an audience
- Finding victory being visible
- Creating real relationships
- Closing them down
- Following up
- Creating an upsell

If you follow this you absolutely WILL make more sales. Take action on each of these steps, and don't just take action, take MASSIVE action!

There are people out there thinking about buying from you. Right now they are thinking if they should buy your product or service or not. It's up to you to get them to buy. With an effective sales strategy, they will buy from you, and they will continue to buy from you.

Don't ever come from a place of lack, when we worry that there isn't enough to go around, or they're going to buy from a different person and not us. If we are trying to sell from a place of lack, that never works. We live in an abundant world, there is plenty to go around. If one sale falls through, there is another one just around the corner.

Selling is an exchange of energy, and our energy is best when we have just made a sale. That is the best time to create another sale, so keep in that positive abundant energy, keep it flowing. If you haven't sold for a while and you're feeling in a bit of a rut, you have to work really hard to get your energy into that place where you're going to make another sale, so remember to bottle it up.

Have a 'sold out' mentality. I remember when I started my first business, and I definitely had a lack mentality. I struggled to get enough customers to make the business viable, let alone sold out. I hustled hard to get customers through the door, and it felt like a lot of effort. I remember the summer of 2013 was when it all started going in the right direction. I was nominated for an award, Young Entrepreneur of the Year, in Essex, where I live. I was absolutely thrilled. I was selling my summer workshops and, for the first time, they were selling without me having to work really hard to get people through the door and it felt good. I was super excited one day as they were coming to interview me for the award, and I had left some other teachers in charge of my theatre school, under strict instruction to tell the children about the upcoming summer holiday workshops. After my interview, I was buzzing and telling my teachers all about it, and one of them said, 'just so you know, about ten people booked in for one of the workshops too'. I couldn't believe it and I immediately added them to my register, and when I did, I realised I had sold 45 spaces. I had always said I was full a 40, but what was an extra 5. I quickly posted everywhere that the workshop was sold out, took the bookings off the website and let everyone know. It was like I had turned a tap on - as soon as I announced it was sold out, everyone wanted to come. I filled that workshop three times over and I learnt that nothing sells out like sold out. And that's when I decided that moving forward in business, I would always have a sold out mentality. And I have! Get yourself into that space where you know you are going to sell out.

When you get to this place where you feel like you make sales easily, it feels so good. And if you think about the beginning of the book when we weren't even on the plane yet, I like to think of this place where the sales are flowing to you easily as being like you're on a private jet - if people want to buy from you, they need to come to you. They're waiting outside your private jet for you to step outside and tell them the doors are open and they can buy from you. You are in control of the sales in your business and it is like you are a magnet for sales, and it's all down to the hard work that you have put in, so celebrate this moment.

COMMIT YOURSELF TO LIFELONG LEARNING

As I already mentioned, we live in a fast-paced world, and social media and the internet has things moving on faster than ever before. As small business owners, we need to be agile, we need to move on with the world and not get stuck in old outdated methods. One way we can do this is by committing ourselves to lifelong learning. I am always reading, learning, listening to podcasts, and consuming as much information about business and sales as I can. I think as long as I live, I will always be learning. I thrive off it and I love it. If you want to be the best salesperson you can possibly be, you need to commit yourself to lifelong learning.

TRUST IN THE PROCESS

Throughout this book, I have spoken about strategy and processes and claimed myself non-woo, and I stand by that! However, I am about to tell you a very woo story which will make you think I'm contradicting myself. I honestly believe that strategy and processes are the things that will drive your business forward. But you do also need to trust in the process, and understand that you have all the tools inside you to do anything you need to.

A few years ago, I was flying to Charleston to attend a business conference and I was so excited. I had dragged my two sisters there and on the way to the airport, I found out that my husband had upgraded all of our tickets to business class. We were beyond hyper and couldn't wait to get checked in and be sipping champagne in the lounge. Now, anybody who has ever travelled to America from the UK will know that you need an ESTA Visa to get in. My brother lives in America, so I have travelled there loads, but when I tried to log into the flight on the way to the airport it said that my ESTA was out of date! Both of my sisters ESTA's were fine, but mine was not. I did a quick search to see how long one took to approve, and the answer was between 60 minutes and 72 hours. What! If it took three days to approve it I would miss the whole conference. I couldn't believe it. We had an hour to go until we reached the airport so I tried to stay positive that this ESTA would come through - but it didn't. I tried to check in, but it wouldn't let me, we waited and waited, until finally I told my sisters to check in and go through the lounge without me. They did, reluctantly. And I waited some more. The lady on the check in desk told me I had 90 minutes and if it didn't come through, I had to go onto a different flight. I had already been waiting for two hours, what were the chances of it coming in?

But at that moment, as far as I could see, I only had one option, and it was to go all woo and believe that this ESTA was coming. I remained positive. I told myself over and over that it was going to come into my inbox before the flight. I visualised it coming in, I meditated on it. The lady on the desk was really lovely and kept checking in on me, I decided to go and buy her a box of chocolates because I wanted to thank her for helping me, and I was still convinced I was getting on the plane, but when I came back, chocolates in hand, there had been a shift change. I still had 20 minutes to go, but the new lady on the desk was not so nice, 'No! You're too late now, you won't make that plane, you'll have to get on another one.' I was gutted. I went to the toilet and cried down the phone to my husband. He said he was going to go and have a look at what our options were. As I hung up the phone, I noticed a notification on my phone. My ESTA had appeared. I ran and ran. I went to a different desk and she told me if I ran, I would make it, I told her I would run as fast as I could and my sisters were about to board the plane as I appeared - it was like something out of a film.

Was it coincidence, or am I slightly woo? I'll let you decide that, but one thing I know for sure is this: staying positive, trusting in the process, and believing it will happen can get you such a long way. Things will be hard along the way, you'll feel like giving up, you'll fail at things, you'll learn lessons, you'll do things differently next time. But what is important is that you keep going, and don't ever give up.

We have reached the end of the book. Well done. I am so grateful that you have picked up this book and read it all, so thank you. Now, go and action all of the chapters in the book. Commit yourself to a killer sales strategy, and it will work time and time again and you'll create raving fans that buy from you time and time again. I know you are committed to being the best you can be at sales, and more than that, you want to do sales the right way, with integrity and with the customers best interests at heart. Go above and beyond and be excellent.

I know that you have it inside you to take your sales to the next level - to get yourself in the top 2% of salespeople will push you forward in your industry. Step into your sales success. You are unstoppable.

ABOUT THE AUTHOR

Charlie Day is a multi award winning entrepreneur. She has built three multi-six-figure businesses from the ground up. Charlie is passionate about helping online business owners create more sales in their businesses, and proclaims that 'selling is easy if you just know how.'

Charlie believes in selling the right way, with integrity and the customers best interests at heart - no sleazy sales tactics or pushy closes with Charlie. She wants to change the face of sales and help people create a sales strategy that works time and time again.

In 2019, at just 31, Charlie won Young Entrepreneur of the Year for Essex; her efforts have been praised by Theo Paphitis when she won Small Business Sunday. Charlie has been featured in The Daily Mail, The Guardian Series, The Independent, The Metro, BBC Radio 2 and Good Morning Britain. She also has a top 50 business podcast, The Entrepreneurs Growth Club.

Charlie teaches people how to create more sales in her Facebook community, The Entrepreneurs Growth Club, and also offers a sales membership, online courses and a mastermind. If you are looking to take your sales to the next level, you can also do 1-2-1 packages with Charlie.

If you are looking for Charlie, you'll usually find her in Costa drinking an Americano, or in Disneyland with her husband and five-year-old, Ernie!

WORK WITH CHARLIE

Yippee!! I would absolutely LOVE for us to connect online. Come and join The Entrepreneurs Growth Club, where I share hints and tips on how to create more sales in your business.

Check out The Entrepreneurs Growth Club podcast on Apple Podcasts, Spotify or Podbean

If you are ready to take your sales to the next level, please visit my website: www.charliedaysales.co.uk

Or feel free to email me charlie@charliedaysales.co.uk

Please, please, please send me a message to let me know that you read my book. Go and drop me a message now.

If you want to download some freebies you can do so here:

https://charliedaysales.co.uk/downloads

 instagram.com/charliedaysales
tiktok.com/@charliedaysales

FINAL WORDS

I have always been a serial goal setter and as part of my goal setting practice, I write ten goals down every day. I have been doing this for three years now, and one of the goals I have been writing on a daily basis is 'I have written a book' (I write the goals as though I have already achieved them to trick the brain into looking for ways to help me achieve them). Three years ago, I had no idea how to write a book, or even where to start. So, a huge thank you to Authors & Co for guiding me through this whole process, it has been fantastic from start to finish. Also a massive thank you to my mentor Lisa Johnson, I wouldn't have written this book without your amazing master-mind and the countless opportunities that you have given me, and a huge thanks for giving me the confidence to get my message out there.

A massive thank you to my mum and dad who have always supported me in whatever I have wanted to do (no matter how crazy). You have taught me the importance of working hard for what you want in life, speaking up, getting myself taught, and celebrating the small things every step of the way.

My amazing sisters Alex and Vicki, who have been a massive part of my journey. My sister Vicki is now the Principal of Little Stars Theatre Workshops, which I set up in 2011, and has grown the business from strength to strength, and Alex is franchisor of Phonics with Robot Reg, which we ran together and learnt so much in the process. They have listened to me talk about business for hours on end, they will help me at the drop of a hat, and I know I wouldn't be where I am today without them. My brother Karl lives all the way in New York but helps me to keep my feet on the ground, even from that distance!

My husband Lewis thought I was mad for wanting to write a book, but he supports me in everything I do, lifts me up when I need it, and cheers me on when I'm moving forward. I know he will always be my biggest supporter.

And for my little Ernie, I hope I can guide the way to showing you that you can do anything that you want to in life if you just put your mind to it.

There are so many people I want to thank from my business life but I couldn't possibly name all of them. Back in 2020 when I set up The Entrepreneurs Growth Club just weeks before the world was hit by a pandemic, I had no idea that this group would change my business (and my life) forever. I became one of those weird people with friends on the internet. Thank you to Davina, my right-hand woman, who listens to all my ideas and actions them immediately, there is no way I would have been able to grow my business to what it is today without you. Thank you to Audrey, who helps me get my message out to the world, and has also supported me from the beginning. Some of the members of The Entrepreneurs Growth Club have been in it since the beginning and still cheer me on today, thank you to Nic Welsh, Sue with the Spoons, Sarah Monte-Colombo, Karen Sidell, and Ruth Tsui, to name a few, who believed in me before I even believed in myself. Lucy Hutchinson from EGC was the first person I shared the book idea with and she gave me the confidence to make it happen. I can't possibly mention everyone, but to each and everyone of The Entrepreneurs Growth Club and my membership, without you this would never have happened. For everyone who joined me for a Thursday coffee morning, or tuned into a Sunday night live, or shared me on #workingmumwednesday, you are the reason I have been able to write my book, so thank you.

Printed in Great Britain
by Amazon

28571366R00076